FROM UPTIGHT TO ALL RIGHT

Strategies for Stress

FROM UPTIGHT TO ALL RIGHT

Strategies for Stress

Jerome Murray, Ph.D.

Manor House Publishing

Published by:
Manor House Publishing
615 Coddingtown Center, Suite 187
Santa Rosa, CA 95401
(707) 538-0377

First Printing – 1987
Second Printing – 1989

Library of Congress Cataloging-in-Publication Data

Murray, Jerome, 1940–
    From uptight to all right.

I. Title.
BF575.S75M86   1987   155.9   87-7762
ISBN 0-942383-06-0

To my wife Sandi

—being with you takes me from "Uptight to All Right"

ACKNOWLEDGEMENTS

I have a debt of gratitude to many people who have helped in making this book possible. It must be expressed.

To Gary Alford for your meticulous scrutiny and helpful comments;

To Gene Hudson for your boundless imagination, your unceasing encouragement, and a magnificent title;

To my patients who taught me so much by sharing their struggles with me;

To all for your friendship;

and to you Sandi—it always comes back to you.

CONTENTS

Chapter One

The Stress Formula

This era has been called "The Age of Anxiety." In fact, we have so much to be anxious about that we could be called "The Uptight Generation." Every day, we are faced with death, destruction, and despair—otherwise known as the daily news! Before we leave the house in the morning, we can have a mild stress reaction just by reading the front page of the newspaper. Technological advances are occurring so fast that we wonder if we can keep up, or if we even want to. We used to just worry about what was happening with our own lives. But now, thanks to the information explosion and the news media, we can worry about what's happening on the other side of the world. As the world gets smaller, our anxieties get larger.

With so many nations having nuclear arsenals, human beings can realistically contemplate the end of the world for the first time in our history. And if we didn't have enough to worry about, now we can worry about stress! Stress has become an important concern to most people, and every time you turn around you see another book or article about the subject. Even though most people are uncomfortably aware that stress can be a problem for them, many still don't understand what it is and what to do about it. Take Oscar, for example.

Oscar was uptight. Here he was sitting in the doctor's office because his wife had insisted that he make an appointment. She knew how he hated going to the doctor. Besides, this wasn't the typical doctor. This was one of those . . . whaddya call 'em? Oh yeah, "shrinks."

He had gone to see ol' "Doc" Murphy at times. "Doc" had been the family physician for years. He wasn't so bad. But after the last examination, Dr. Murphy had recommended that he make an appointment with this new guy. The "Shrink." Once his wife heard that "Doc" Murphy said it was really important, there was no way out of it.

Oscar began to think of the symptoms which caused him to see "Doc" Murphy originally. He had thought at first that something was wrong with his heart. He could feel it pounding at times. That didn't seem right. His neck and lower back had been hurting as well, so a visit to "Doc" Murphy had seemed like a good idea.

But his wife was worried about other things. She thought he was too nervous and uptight. It's true he'd been real tense and unable to relax for some time now, but there was a lot of pressure in his job. He'd been promoted and was certain some of his former associates were jealous of him. He felt that one of them had been "bad-mouthing" him to his new staff. Production was down, they hadn't been giving him the respect he deserved, and the jealousy and "bad-mouthing" was probably the cause. He was sure of it. Oscar decided to make sure his boss knew the real reason for the poor performance in his section. Otherwise, the boss might think it was because he couldn't handle his job.

But he had always been able to handle pressure before. He couldn't see how his physical concerns had anything to do with his job. This must be something else. Maybe it was because of all the criticism he had been taking from his wife lately. His marriage wasn't a storybook marriage. Whose marriage was? He knew that he could improve in a lot of areas, but that was no reason for his wife to be overreacting. She had even threatened divorce. He just didn't need her complaining; he had enough to worry about.

Oscar's mind was getting confused from all these problems. There was too much pressure. Concentration had been difficult, and he found himself daydreaming a lot and forgetting what he was doing or where he was . . . and he was so tired all the time. It was confusing. He was tired, but he couldn't get to sleep. When he did sleep, it was fitful and restless.

"I must be getting older," he thought. "Because I just don't have any energy or any fun anymore." The truth was he didn't even have energy for sex. And when his mind seemed to be in the mood for sex, his body had other ideas. That really disturbed him.

Once in a while, Oscar felt, well . . . frightened. He wasn't frightened of anything he was aware of—just scared. His palms would sweat, his pulse would race, and he felt as if he had to urinate. His chest sure hurt. Right there near his heart, too. It was a weird feeling. Sometimes he thought he might be having a heart attack.

He knew he had been eating and smoking too much. The "Doc" didn't have to tell him that. He could see it and feel it. But his wife was wrong about the drinking. Oscar was convinced he could handle the booze. Besides, he needed it to relax. He knew when to quit. Oscar reminded himself that he wasn't as bad as some of the guys at the office. They were using amphetamines and snorting cocaine. He hadn't stooped to that, he thought proudly.

What was that problem "Doc" Murphy thought he had? A stress reaction? What was that? A new disease? Didn't everyone have a little stress? Did "Doc" think he was a weakling or something?

As he sat waiting for his appointment, he thought, "I don't know what this shrink is going to say, but I probably won't like it . . . ."

With all the recent attention being given to the subject, it does seem as if stress is a newly discovered disease. But Oscar's problem is all too common. In fact, stress is as old as the human race. The only difference is, we now have a new word to describe our old problems. And what problems! The list includes almost every diagnostic label.

Stress is a causative or aggravating factor in peptic ulcers, colitis, migraine and tension headaches, hypertension, athero-sclerosis, rheumatoid arthritis—just to name a few. It has even been implicated in certain types of cancer. It has been estimated that over fifty percent of our health complaints are related to stress.

Not impressed yet? Then think of it this way. Out of the top ten causes of death, only one is an infectious disease. The other nine all involve some degree of stress.

Aside from these physical concerns, stress is a major consider-ation in mental and emotional disorders. Every mental health professional knows that chronic tension (being uptight) not only leads to the physical symptoms found in psychosomatic and psy-chophysiological disorders, but can also distort judgment and reason, resulting in disorganized, inappropriate behavior. Stress reactions (being uptight) can turn a loving friend into an angry stranger.

And are we uptight? Are we ever! After all, the United States is a society where the most frequently prescribed drug is a tran-quilizer.

The more we learn about stress, the more we learn how per-vasive is its influence. We have known for a while that stress can have a negative effect on physical and mental health. That knowl-edge fails to alarm some people, however, who tend to feel that they are immortal or immune from the consequences of stress.

If that describes you, here's a little "attention-getter." Stress is hitting you right in your pocketbook! It's not just your physical health that is in jeopardy, but your fiscal health as well. Industry analysts are now claiming that the ravages of stress extend to America's sacred cow—the Gross National Product. Now that's serious!

According to the U.S. Clearinghouse for Mental Health Information, productivity losses over the last few years caused by stress-related physical diseases are approaching 75 billion dollars. Add to that the losses in productivity resulting from mental disorders, and the figure is closer to 100 billion dollars!

This loss of productivity is bad enough, but that's not all. Not only does stress cause productivity to go down, it makes costs go up. For many corporations, health benefits and disability payments have become the largest slice of their operating costs pie.

Even the most cynical observer would agree that the long-standing concern with alcoholism and the more recent increase in drug use in the corporate world are related to stress. This understanding, added to the new awareness of the economics of stress, is inducing many companies to sit up and take notice. Some of the leading corporations in America are discovering that an ounce of prevention is a lot cheaper than a pound of cure.

It's not just a problem for the United States. All industrialized nations have steadily increasing problems related to stress. These facts make it a big concern—you can get uptight just thinking about it. Yet with all the evidence of how serious a problem stress can be, it is something that we can't and shouldn't eliminate. Our relationship with stress is similar to the one some people tell me they have with their spouses—they can't live with them, and they can't live without them.

As we will elaborate on later, stress is essential to our mental and physical health even though it is also a major threat. Effective strategies for coping with stress do not have as their objective the elimination of stress. Stress is inevitable and even necessary. The problem then is not stress, but how we handle stress.

The various stressors we face in normal living may act in the manner of an exercise that tones up our bodies and builds muscle tissue, permitting greater feats of strength. Stress can stimulate growth and confidence and, within tolerable levels, can actually serve to keep us alive. Stress only becomes a problem when it exceeds our ability to cope with it, and especially if it remains at high levels for long periods of time.

When stress is not managed effectively, it causes "distress," and that's the problem. "Distress" is what we want to avoid, not stress. Learning to identify what stress is will enable you to devise coping strategies that prevent *stress* from becoming "distress."

You may already be familiar with several techniques for coping with stress. There are plenty of books that teach stress-coping techniques intended to reduce the severity of "distress." But, techniques for reducing "distress" are not enough. You need to have strategies for preventing stress from becoming "distress" in the first place. These strategies should be based on fundamental principles for dealing with stress, and should give you the level of knowledge that will enable you to increase your resilience to stress.

But before I start describing specific strategies for stress, it is important to understand what stress really is. With a sound grasp of these concepts, you will be able to use the strategies much more effectively. Techniques are based on strategies, and strategies require a thorough understanding of stress. Since developing strategies for stress is the goal, we need to better understand stress.

WHAT IS STRESS?

If stress is so important to our well-being, why do so few people understand what it is? We have a superficial idea of what it is: long lines at the bank, slowpokes driving forty in the fast lane, more outgo than income, and, of course, mothers-in-law (but then, in-laws have their own idea of what stress is).

Everyone has a candidate to nominate as their greatest source of stress, and the list ranges from gripes about toothpaste squeezed in the middle to the fear of nuclear annihilation. Some even advertise their beliefs on bumper stickers and T-shirts. A lot of parents seem to agree with one I see frequently: "Insanity is inherited; you get it from your kids."

Stress does come in a variety of packages, but it's a little more complicated than a list of pet peeves. Actually, none of these things is an example of stress. Rather, they are stressors. A stressor is a situation or event that produces stress.

While you may have a very clear picture of the things that produce stress in you, it is probable that you don't really understand what the stressors are doing to you. What they are doing is called stress, and if you don't have an effective strategy for it, it becomes "distress."

THE FIGHT-OR-FLIGHT SYNDROME

A description of the "fight-or-flight" syndrome has become a cliché in discussions of stress. It is so frequently used to explain stress reactions that you are probably already aware of it. But, just in case you aren't fully aware of the fundamental role it plays in stress, some illustration and expansion of the concept is warranted.

The "fight-or-flight" syndrome refers to the body's innate response to a perceived threat. Whenever a danger is perceived, your body begins to automatically prepare you to deal with that danger. For instance, if you saw a car just about to strike you on a street, the "fight-or-flight" syndrome would immediately go into effect.

The moment the danger is perceived, your adrenal glands pump large amounts of adrenaline into your bloodstream. This is the beginning of a massive mobilization of your body's defensive resources. Stored sugar is fed into the blood for increased energy. Your red blood cell count rises in preparation for strenuous muscle activity. Your heart beats faster, and your pulse rate and blood pressure increase.

This dramatic change in your blood's circulation allows more oxygen to be transported throughout the body, as well as improving the rate of carbon dioxide removal. The lungs help out by expanding the capacity of the small air sacs called alveoli. The blood's ability to clot is enhanced, and it is diverted from the peripheral areas of the body to inhibit possible blood loss during the emergency. It is then forced into the vital organs, where it is most needed, by the dilation and contraction of appropriate blood vessels. Routine stomach contractions are inhibited, stopping digestion, and, if you just ate, the food sits like a rock in your stomach.

These are just a few of the things the body does to prepare itself for any eventuality provoked by the emergency. All of these body changes are intended to prepare you to deal quickly and immediately with an emergency situation. They are normal and perfectly acceptable, providing that the emergency is real, immediate, and short-term. Because of these body changes, you can fight the danger or escape from it as needed. But what happens when you can't do either? You have to adjust to it. If you don't make an effective adjustment, the preparatory responses continue unabated, playing havoc with your body.

Animals, placed in a situation which they cannot fight and from which they cannot flee, will sometimes simply die from the stress. Caribou were caught in Newfoundland and caged with the goal of re-introducing them into northern Maine. Several of the caribou were found dead upon their arrival in Maine. Because they were caged, they were unable to fight or escape, and the stress of their capture killed them. They couldn't adjust. Ironically, that is exactly the kind of stress many people are living with daily.

Not all stressors are real, immediate, and short-term. The stress of modern society is a little more complex than having to jump out of the way of an oncoming vehicle, and that is precisely why we have stress problems.

Our problems today aren't ones that can be easily escaped from or fought. They are complex and confusing. Like the caribou, we are trapped in a cage.

TRAPPED!

There are many traps in which you can be caught. A troubled marriage can trap you. A partner who won't acknowledge the need for change prevents you from "fighting" the problem; and social pressures, moral restraints, and economic concerns can prevent you from "fleeing." You are trapped!

An unsatisfying job that offers no chance for growth can be a cage. Unfulfilled, you long for change. But the prospects of being without work and unable to support yourself or your family trap you. Any troubling situation which you feel unable to change and from which you can't escape is a trap. Here are some typical traps:

> *1. The Phantom Trap* Not all our problems are real; some of them are imagined. Many people live under constant stress because of unrealistic fears. Since the fears are phantoms, these people can't fight against or flee from them. They are trapped by the phantoms of what could happen, or might happen, and become crippled by stress.

> *2. The Ambiguity Trap* Our problems are not always clear, tangible dangers, such as an onrushing car. Most of them are intangible and ambiguous, as with a concern for personal meaning and values. Lacking a sense of direction and having no clarity to our values can be debilitating, and it's not a problem that can be escaped from or fought. Trapped again.

3. The Hidden Trap The cause of our "distress" isn't always apparent; it may only be implied and we can't readily identify the source. Threats to self-esteem can be paralyzing but may have no specific focus for our coping efforts. Without an identifiable hazard to fight against or flee from, we once more feel trapped.

4. The Endurance Trap Most of our stress problems today involve having to handle long-term predicaments instead of short-term emergencies. Marital tribulations, child-raising anxieties, occupational pressures, and financial hardships can trap us for years and produce unrelenting stress.

5. The Velvet Trap Some stressful situations may trap us with their velvet linings. One of my patients stayed in a marriage for years in a relationship that was systematically destroying her self-esteem and health. She was trapped by her unwillingness to confront her problems and run the risk of losing the comfort and luxury supplied by her wealthy husband.

All of these traps put us in situations which prolong the stress, and prolonged stress is deadly. The fact that much of our stress is long-term rather than short-term accounts for the prevalence of stress-related psychosomatic disorders. Short-term stress is relatively easy to cope with and recover from, but long-term, uninterrupted stress is devastating. It invariably results in some degree of physical and psychological deterioration.

When the stress is short-term and the response is immediate, the previously described body changes rapidly return to normal. They may even drop below the pre-emergency baseline levels. Your system balances out and you return to business as usual with few, if any, residual complications.

Without the opportunity to return to normal baseline levels as with long-term stress, your body becomes accustomed to higher and higher baseline levels of physiological preparedness. In time, such things as blood pressure and pulse rate remain permanently elevated. You're all dressed up, but there's nowhere to go!

THE GENERAL ADAPTATION SYNDROME

When you are experiencing unrelenting stress, your body will react in a predictable manner. Hans Selye discovered the process in the 1930s. Dr. Selye, the patron saint of stress research, was motivated to do his pioneer studies on stress by his experiences as an intern.

While making the rounds in a teaching hospital with a group of his peers, he made a simple, yet profound, observation. In spite of the varied diagnoses given to the patients, he observed that they all had one thing in common—they all "looked sick." He proposed that underlying each disease there was a "syndrome of sickness" common to all. It was his belief that no matter how unique the illness might be, the body made the same nonspecific response to each disease.

In his verifying research, Selye discovered that when the body is attacked by either a physical or psychological stressor, it always responds in a predictable manner. The name he gave this response was *The General Adaptation Syndrome,* with the unfortunate acronym of GAS.

ALARM, RESISTANCE, AND EXHAUSTION

When an individual's coping behavior fails to handle a stressor or group of stressors, integrated functioning is reduced, leading to an eventual breakdown of the body and personality. This process, or General Adaptation Syndrome, typically occurs in

11

three phases: the Alarm phase, the Resistance phase, and the Exhaustion phase.

To illustrate this syndrome, consider the hypothetical case of a person we will call Ted. This isn't a real story, but it could be.

> *1. The Alarm Phase* Ted just received word that management was considering laying him off. He wasn't sure of the company's motive. He had heard varying stories as to the reasons for his layoff, ranging from his lack of competence to company cutbacks resulting from the poor economy. Ted didn't know the reason. The only thing he knew for certain was that he could not afford to lose his job. His marriage was already shaky and, with his wife expecting a baby, their relationship didn't need another setback, let alone a financial one.
>
> In the Alarm phase Ted's body mobilized its defenses (as in the "fight-or-flight" syndrome) in preparation for coping with the stressor. This is a time of generalized excitation and alertness. There is increased arousal and tension (in other words, Ted got uptight), combined with heightened sensitivity, vigilance, and determined efforts at self-control.
>
> It is during the Alarm phase that the effectiveness of our coping strategies becomes apparent. If our adjustment is effective, no symptoms develop. When the adjustment is ineffective, symptoms of maladjustment begin to appear such as chronic anxiety and tension, gastrointestinal or other physical disorders, and decreased efficiency.

Since Ted wasn't coping well, he experienced trouble sleeping, chronic indigestion, and increased irritability. His mind was filled with competing thoughts and his concentration lapsed. This preoccupation resulted in a poorer performance on the job, further aggravating his original concerns.

2. *The Resistance Phase* As the situation producing the stress continued, Ted's reactions moved into the Resistance phase. During this phase, there is usually increased rigidity — as Ted tries to "hang in there," like a drowning man clinging to a straw. Too much stress narrows the perceptual field, limiting attention and the range of responsiveness.

Ted became preoccupied with his problems and was unaware and inattentive to other areas of his life. His tunnel vision narrowed his perception of circumstances and left him unable to keep his perspective. Spontaneity and the ability to relax were replaced with a tense, driven attitude. Ted was drinking more in an effort to unwind, which only worsened the ulcer he was developing.

The rigidity associated with this phase prevents a reassessment of the situation, which could lead to the use of more effective coping strategies. The strain becomes obvious and commonly includes the development of psychosomatic symptoms.

Ted still has the opportunity to make a successful adjustment to his problems, thereby ending the cycle. The length of time before the stress reaction ends is directly related to the intensity of the stressors and Ted's coping ability. However, since Ted was still not coping effectively, his rigidity precluded a change of coping strategy, and the stress reaction continued. If a successful adjustment is not made, the third and final phase begins.

3. *The Exhaustion Phase* Ted was now in obvious trouble. Everyone knew it, including him. His drinking became excessive; his angry outbursts isolated him from friends and family; nagging suspicions prompted hostile accusations against people he felt were persecuting him; and he hit his wife when she attempted to confront him with his deterioration. He became depressed and withdrawn, lost his job, his family, and his health.

During the Exhaustion phase, decompensation escalates. Coping attempts become exaggerated, frantic, and inappropriate. The pattern may involve such symptoms as "psychotic breaks" or metabolic changes in the brain associated with delusions and hallucinations, stuporous apathy, and even uncontrolled violence.

The decompensation or breakdown can be physical, mental, or both. If the stressor continues unabated, the ultimate stress reaction can occur—death!

THE STRESS FORMULA: F + R = S

While this oversimplified description of the General Adaptation Syndrome explains some of our reactions to stress, it still doesn't define stress.

To really understand stress, you must, as Dr. Selye did, look to the seemingly unrelated field of mechanical engineering. From that discipline we derive the formula that best defines stress. Force plus Resistance equals Stress; or put symbolically, F + R = S. Consider this application of the formula in mechanical engineering. The Force part of the formula is represented by the impact of vehicular traffic going across a bridge. The Resistance part is represented by the strength of the steel girders in the bridge; and the effect on the bridge is Stress.

It is obvious, then, that when the impact of the vehicles (the Force) exceeds the strength of the steel girders (the Resistance), it produces a serious strain (Distress) on the bridge. If this strain is not reduced, it could lead to a collapse of the bridge which, in human terms, means sickness and death.

But how does this translate into the psychological stress of our everyday lives? To understand that, think of Force as being any adjustment demand made on you. Anything that requires you to adjust from your usual style of coping is an adjustment demand. Resistance refers to your inability or unwillingness to change your characteristic pattern of coping with adjustment demands. Each of these concepts will be examined and explained one at a time.

All of the strategies in this book are based on three principles for living with stress: 1. Building an immune system for stress, 2. Increasing your stress-survival quotient, and 3. Coping with "distress." Much has been written about coping with "distress," but not much has been said about how to keep it from happening. *Learning how to deal with the symptoms of stress is not stress management.* Successful stress management means knowing how to handle stress effectively so that it does not become *"distress."* The total avoidance of "distress" in your life is probably impossible, but minimizing it is definitely possible, and that's what stress management is all about.

The primary intent of this book is to teach you how to increase your resilience to stress, thereby minimizing "distress" in your life. Learning techniques to help you after you are already in "distress" is important. But building a stress-resilient personality

15

that keeps stress from becoming "distress" is even more important.

But first things first. You need to make sure your immune system for stress is functioning well before you do anything else.

If you are "Uptight," just hang on; we are heading for "All Right"!

Chapter Two

Building
an Immune System
for Stress

Adjustment demands, the "Force" of our Stress Formula, are a fact of life. They aren't going to go away, nor should they. That would indeed be a dull world. It is impossible and even undesirable to eliminate them, so if we are to survive in a world of challenge and change, we need to increase our resistance to the barrage of stressors that bombard us daily.

An ineffective but all too common strategy for stress is to wait until we are in a condition of "distress" and then try to use techniques such as vacations and relaxation to combat the negative effects. Techniques for dealing with "distress" are important, but often are too little, too late.

There are many "techniques" for dealing with "distress" that you will learn or that you already know. None of these, however, is a substitute for having a solid, underlying, stress-resilient structure to your personality. The most effective strategies are those centering around techniques that build a healthy body and mind. Closing the barn door before the horses get out makes more sense than chasing the horses.

You will learn in the later chapters how to build a stress-resilient personality by increasing your stress-survival quotient. This chapter concerns an even more basic issue — having an immune system for stress. Just as health techniques for improving your physical health aren't ultimately effective if your immune system isn't working, a stress-resilient personality can't stay that way if your personality's immune system makes you vulnerable to stress.

Build a stress-resilient personality using the concepts in this book. But remember that it will profit you nothing if your immune system is not functioning.

THE IMMUNE SYSTEM CALLED LOVING

There is a terrible disease called AIDS. It is characterized by a breakdown of the body's immunological system. At this point, there is no cure. Even with a perfectly healthy body, once an individual has AIDS they are helpless to resist disease. Similarly, no matter how healthy a person's mind and body, there must also be a healthy immune system to resist stress. Without the ability to fight off "dis-ease," death is inevitable.

This physical analogy can be correlated with how you deal with stress. The stress-resilient structure to your personality is like the skeleton of your body. "Distress-reducing" techniques are like its muscles. If the skeleton is weak, it makes no difference how strong the muscles are; the body will collapse under pressure. If both are strong, it is still not enough to save you if your immune system is not working. Similarly, all the stress-reducing "techniques" in the world cannot sustain you in the absence of warm, loving relationships.

That brings us to the first strategy for stress.

The first and most important strategy for stress has to do with your need for nearness.

Stress Strategy #1

The ability to create and maintain loving relationships is the single best thing you can do to stressproof your personality.

To understand more about this, take a look at the Holmes-Rahe scale on page 40. I'll explain this scale in more detail later, but, for now, just take a look at it.

As you look over the Holmes-Rahe scale, you will find that a disproportionate number of stressors are associated with marriage. Living in harmony with another person necessitates a considerable amount of adjusting. For a relationship to promote growth and mutual satisfaction, there must be mutual accommodation.

While getting into marriage is stressful, getting out is even more stressful. Separation and divorce are particularly damaging, rated at 65 and 73 Life Change Units respectively. When you see all the stressors associated with marriage and you note that a minor violation of the law is worth a mere 11 LCUs, you may arrive at an alarming conclusion: you're better off being in trouble with the law than being married!

Ignoring the levity, there is actually a far more illuminating inference to be drawn from that fact.

Examine the first five stressors on the list. They are, in order: Death of a spouse, Divorce, Marital separation, Jail term, and Death of a close family member. These are the five most stressful events a human being can experience. Do you notice anything that they all have in common?

Like many others, I've thought a lot about what makes people happy and fulfilled. It seems obvious that people can only be fulfilled when some basic need or needs are met. I've studied dozens of philosophies that purported to tell what man's basic needs were. I've encountered everything from the elaborate and complex explanations of some belief systems to the cynical postulations of nihilism. Wise minds have spent lifetimes trying to deduce the inner workings of the human psyche, and the effort to understand, at times, may seem fruitless.

Yet, in the middle of this perplexing question, one thing seems apparent. In the search to discover man's basic psychological needs, it would appear to follow logically that—whatever they are—being deprived of them would be highly stressful.

With that in mind, it is most enlightening to discover that the five most stressful events a human being can experience all have the same thing in common—separation from loved ones. This would suggest that our basic psychological needs are met in loving, bonded attachments.

More and more health specialists are accepting the position that disrupted social bonds somehow affect the body's immune system, increasing susceptibility to disease. The specific disease contracted appears to be determined by other risk factors. But increased vulnerability to disease is definitely associated with broken relationships and social isolation.

Consider the following findings from the California Department of Mental Health that illustrate the correlation between social ties and health.

1. People who isolate themselves from others have from two to four times the risk of premature death.

2. Terminal cancer strikes isolated people more often than it does those with bonded relationships.

3. The rates of mental hospitalization are five to ten times greater for separated, divorced, and widowed persons than for married people.

4. Pregnant women under stress and without supportive relationships have three times the number of complications than pregnant women with close ties who are equally stressed.

5. Women who can confide in a close friend are much less likely to become depressed.

Studies have indicated that the mortality rate of widowers is from forty to sixty percent higher during the first six months of bereavement. If remarriage occurs, mortality rates go back down to normal.

The health-risk vulnerability of people lacking committed social bonds is further dramatized by a study examining death rates for smokers and non-smokers. Not surprisingly, smokers have higher death rates than non-smokers. But, in both smoking and non-smoking populations, single, widowed, and divorced men had the highest death rates. Divorced men who smoked had the highest death rates of all.

If the loss of established relationships produces the greatest stress, then the establishment of loving, committed relationships is our greatest safeguard against stress. The "Catch-22" is that while relationships provide our richest source of satisfaction, they also provide a great potential for stress because they require much adjustment.

There is no question that trying to have successful relationships with one person in particular, or people in general, can be frustrating and stressful. Some people have concluded that it's not even worth the trouble. They organize their lives so they have minimum contact with others. This can take the simple and direct form of choosing a job and lifestyle that don't require much contact with others, to the extreme of a hermit-like existence where all contact with people is avoided.

A far more common strategy for putting distance between ourselves and others is to erect emotional barriers. These barriers can be quite effective at keeping others from getting too close. If you've ever been hurt in a relationship, you can have some sympathy for people who fear letting others get too close. But it doesn't really work. You merely trade one set of problems for another. And the problems you create for yourself by isolation are far worse than the ones caused by relationships.

Aside from the fact that contact with people on our populous planet is inevitable, it is essential to our well-being. A great number of studies indicate just how essential contact with others is, suggesting that our most basic need may be the need for nearness.

THE NEED FOR NEARNESS

There is ample evidence that our vulnerability to stress is intensified by the lack of close, bonded relationships. Illustrations abound which confirm that we derive something from attachments that, in effect, serve to immunize us against stress.

This need that I call the need for nearness is manifested in our striving to feel wanted, needed, and valued. The need for nearness is met through the establishment of intimate social bonds, and involves such things as a sense of belonging, feeling wanted, needed, desired, and loved. Even the need for self-esteem is an expression of the need for nearness. When we feel good about ourselves, it increases our belief that we are worthy of belonging. Feeling worthy of being wanted by someone increases our assurance of meeting our needs for nearness.

Marriage and family have historically been our greatest resources for belonging and attachment. In an age when more people are uptight then ever before, it comes as no surprise that marriages and families are less secure then ever before. It almost seems that broken families are the rule and not the exception.

The fact is, the institution of marriage and family simply does not offer the stability and support it once did.

You're probably already aware that married people live longer than single people. We simply don't do as well alone as we do when we feel attachment. As the divorce rate escalates, so does our vulnerability to stress. Those of you who think that marriage is leading a "dog's life" should consider this. Senior citizens who live with pets live longer than those who live alone. It would appear that a dog is better than nothing.

However, don't get too engrossed analyzing the relative virtues of marriage. The evidence of our need for attachments is not limited to marriage, and the message here is more basic. In order to maximize our potential for productive living, we need to feel wanted, needed, and attached. We need nearness. And it appears that we are born with this need.

ISOLATION VS. NEARNESS

Harlow's classic study showed that monkeys raised in isolation developed abnormally. They became abnormal socially and sexually, and were grossly deficient as parents. It was apparent that some attachment with the mother monkey was required for healthy development.

Harlow's experiment sought to determine whether a monkey was attached to its mother because she was a source of food, or if it needed the nearness for its own sake. Two surrogate "mothers" made out of wire and shaped to look like monkeys were used. One was simply a wire frame with a nipple providing nourishment. The other had no source of food but was covered with terry-cloth, making "her" cuddly.

The results were dramatic. No matter which "mother" was the source of food, the infant monkey spent all of its time clinging to the "cuddly" mother. The infant monkey's craving for the cuddly nearness of the terry-cloth "mother" was for more than mere comfort. When permitted to have the attachment to the cuddly mother, the young monkey's development proceeded along normal parameters. Food is important, but food alone will not produce a healthy monkey or child.

Once a monkey has established a relationship with a real mother, the effects of separation are impressive. The first response to separation is agitation, lack of sleep, restlessness, fingersucking, and crying. Within days, the response changes to withdrawn, apathetic behavior. Prolonged separation can permanently distort the developing personality.

There is no evidence that an adjustment to separation will occur with repeated separations. The absence of early loving attachments can leave permanent scars on development. There would appear to be no substitute for the need for nearness in healthy development.

Before you come to the conclusion that I am trying to make a monkey out of you, consider this. The same kind of developmental deficiencies occur with human infants when they are denied nearness. Furthermore, there is no requirement that the attachment has to be with the mother. Infants don't discriminate by gender, and will blossom just as well attached to a father as to a mother. When both parents are present, the ideal for the child, of course, is attachment to both mother and father.

THE MYSTERY CALLED MARASMUS

In years past, observers were baffled by the fact that some infants deteriorated physically in spite of what they felt was adequate caretaking. The condition came to be known as marasmus or "the wasting disease." Those afflicted by marasmus experience a slow and progressive deterioration, both physically and psychologically, that can result in their death.

Marasmus is a little-known condition that is caused by emotional neglect. It affects both the very young and the very old when they are ignored by the group in between.

For years, it was observed that babies in orphanages had a higher mortality rate than children living in intact families. The babies in orphanages had satisfactory physical care but received almost no touching or holding. When this was remedied by regular holding and caressing periods, their mortality rates went down.

Babies need much more than changing and feeding. Technically competent caretaking alone is not sufficient to ensure that a child will develop normally. Babies need more than that; they need to be held and stroked. Fortunately, most parents also have a need to do this. Holding an infant stimulates an almost instinctual need to stroke and caress the child. As a baby is held and caressed, it is as if a message penetrates deep into the child's subconscious that it is wanted and loved. Without this physical contact, children die. Even if they do not die physically, part of them can die psychologically. Cold, mechanical parenting combined with the absence of touching has been implicated in certain types of childhood autism and schizophrenia. Without the perception of being wanted, and without the feeling of being loved, our sense of personhood struggles vainly to survive. And, even if it does survive, it becomes distorted and disorganized. The result is a substantial vulnerability to stress.

In a study of 157 exceptionally well adjusted children, the researchers found no correlation between the type of discipline used by the parents, and the level of adjustment. The only similar characteristic of all the well-adjusted children was that the children reported feeling loved and wanted by their parents. Notice the wording. The essential factor was not that the parents *said* they loved and wanted their children, but that the children *felt* loved and wanted. It's not enough to say it; the message has to reach the child and be accepted. When it does, it is a powerful force for mental health. It always will be.

We never lose the need to feel wanted and loved. It may become well hidden through neglect or fear, but we never lose it.

From cradle to grave, the need for nearness is demonstrated in almost everything we do. While we never outgrow our need for concrete indications that we are wanted and loved, we also look for more abstract manifestations as we grow older. Even such seemingly irrelevant things as being asked our opinion or getting a pay raise can signal that we are a valued member of the group. Anything that makes us feel more worthy becomes an assurance that we are worthy of belonging, and we are comforted.

LOVING WELL AND LIVING LONGER

In recent years, there has been much publicity regarding people who have lived past one hundred years of age. Social scientists have traversed the world to study small, unique societies that are characterized by an above-average percentage of centenarians. Upon discovering one of these groups, they naturally want to determine why these people live longer than the rest of us. There must be a little of Ponce de Leon in all of us because we are more than a trifle curious as to the results of that research. But, then, it's only natural to want to live longer and better.

Any social scientist worth his salt is constantly on the alert for an interesting subject for a book. It's not surprising that when one of these antediluvian groups is located, the bookstores soon bulge with volumes about them.

Remember the first group of centenarians they found in Russia? Discovering that these ancients continued to lead active, vigorous lives, even into advanced years, caused a health revolution. Everyone jumped on the fitness bandwagon, and the bookstores were flooded with volumes on jogging, walking, and other methods of staying cardiovascularly fit. Exercise fanatics were convinced that fitness was the magic elixir of perpetual youth, and Adidas loved it.

The second band of aged ones that was studied was not characterized by much activity. What a letdown! Here was a group of people down in India living to be past one hundred years of age and they hardly ever moved. Their long lives were obviously not precipitated by exercise. Undaunted, the researchers kept looking for the cause of their longevity.

They soon discovered that while it was true this bunch didn't move much, they did have a unique diet. It consisted of foods high in fiber. Yeah, you guessed it! An avalanche of essays inundated us on diet, nutrition, and the wonders of fiber!

It was the third passel of senior citizens discovered in South America that proved to be a puzzler. They didn't exercise much, and their diet wasn't particularly interesting. While diet and exercise are certainly important contributors to living longer, they aren't enough. This latest group couldn't be explained by diet and exercise alone. Pondering this question, the researchers wondered if there was another variable common to all long-lived populations. It was concluded there must be, and they set out to find the common denominator.

Although this current bevy of oldsters posed a problem, these persistent literati knew there was a book hiding in there somewhere. And then someone made a brilliant deduction. As each group of centenarians was compared, the missing ingredient for each case of longevity became apparent.

In every instance, the community valued and respected its older generation. There was no mandatory retirement age, no convalescent homes—in fact, no segregation of any kind. They weren't put out to pasture as they got older. Instead, they were involved in activities of the community, including meaningful work. They were valued for their experience and knowledge and made to feel a part of the fabric of the community. In short, rather than being put on the shelf to vegetate until death, these old-timers felt needed, wanted, and loved!

In order to live, we must want to live. To want to live, we must have a reason. That reason is found when we feel wanted and needed by others.

But what does this have to do with stress?

The healing and nurturing power of loving and being loved resounds through all of our experience. Pressure, frustration, and tension dissolve in the arms of someone you love. You cannot be loving and uptight at the same time.

Every technique you may use to fight disease is handicapped if your body's immunological system is dysfunctional. To fight disease, you first need a healthy, well-functioning immune system. Dealing with stress follows the same pattern. Learn and use all the techniques this book, or any other source, can teach you. But keep first things first. Make sure that your priority is to keep your immune system in good repair.

Here are some nearness-building techniques that will help expand the connectedness in your relationships. Use these as idea-magnifiers that springboard you into creating your own techniques.

1. When it is not possible to be together, write short notes of care and support to each other and leave them in special places. Or, make short "thinking of you" telephone calls.

2. Make bedtime a special time of the day. Share the day's experiences, read a continuing story to younger children, share a prayer time, or give a backrub to someone you love.

3. Develop family customs and traditions that have special meaning for everyone. Saying grace at meals, the way birthdays and holidays are celebrated, special nights of the week that are family nights or husband-wife nights—these are just a few of the possibilities.

4. Make mealtime an important time. Eat as a family at least twice a week with the television off. Minimize distractions and don't discuss problems. Talk about positive, uplifting topics.

5. Have family councils to discuss family concerns. Let everyone be heard with no criticisms or putdowns allowed.

If you are without the advantage of family, adapt the suggestions to your support group. Make them family.

Acknowledging your need for nearness will allow you to find opportunities to nourish and strengthen your personality's immune system. That immune structure is the ability to give and receive love. It is built by nourishing the need for nearness, and it is not difficult to deduce that our need for nearness is most satisfied in loving relationships.

The message is clear. If there is an immune system for stress, it thrives when we are loving and being loved.

Chapter Three

The "Force" Is With Us

Change is both unavoidable and essential but, when a change occurs that requires skills not readily available, stress results. Even greater stress accrues if the change that occurs is faster than our ability to adjust to it. We just can't keep up and a stress overload results, with an inevitable physical or psychological breakdown.

Every day, we make adjustments in our thinking and behavior, as required by the circumstances in our lives. Most of these adjustments are unconscious, as we automatically make adjustments to routine daily living requirements, drawing from our repertoire of coping techniques. There is negligible stress from these routine adjustments since our skill and experience level make these adjustments smooth and simple.

Just as we learn skills in order to do a job, we also learn skills for coping with the demands life makes on us. Similarly, the number and effectiveness of these skills vary from person to person. In life, as on the job, some people have many skills that are highly effective, while others have limited, marginally effective skills.

When a situation occurs requiring skills beyond our normal range of coping skills, we call it an adjustment demand. In other words, any situation that requires you to adjust, or deviate, from your usual style of coping is an adjustment demand. It may also be an adjustment demand if it occurs infrequently and our skill dealing with it is rusty and not easily applied.

In general, adjustment demands may be classified into three categories: Frustration, Conflict, and Pressure.

Frustration   Frustration occurs whenever we are blocked, or thwarted, from pursuing an objective. The inability to proceed, temporarily or permanently, toward a desired objective will always produce frustration. When we are prevented from achieving a goal, frustration makes the implicit demand to adjust to a different method or a different goal. Delays, lacks, losses, failures, and even guilt can all cause frustration.

As with conflict and pressure, the source of frustration may be within us or within our environment. Frustration can be caused by environmental conditions such as rain falling on a carefully planned picnic, to the more serious events like earthquakes, famine, pestilence, and floods.

In between are a host of different frustrations that all demand coping ability. Flat tires on the way to work, bureaucratic red tape, children who won't behave, a hostile and jealous supervisor, lovers who won't love, financial limitations, drivers going fifty in the fast lane, and a thousand more that can push us over the brink if we lack adequate coping skills.

The kind of person we are can also keep us from getting what we want. Physical handicaps, disease, low intelligence, inadequate competencies, and an irritating personality can frustrate us through our own limitations. Immaturity, personal rigidity, and a cold interpersonal style can also be sources of frustration that leave us perpetually angry.

Frustration demands the adjustment of changing our objective or the method used to obtain the objective. That may be task enough by itself, but it is complicated by frustration's by-product. The innate, immediate reaction to frustration is aggression, and the inability to cope with aggressive, angry feelings leads to much suffering.

Aggression alone is not bad because it provides extra energy and the impetus to break through the frustration and achieve the goal. But, when the aggression overrides the analytic thinking necessary to evaluate the problem, or when the aggression is inappropriately expressed in hostile, destructive ways, then it becomes a problem. And what a problem! Misdirected, destructively expressed aggression causes more frustration, and the cycle of frustration-aggression leads downward.

The basic techniques for coping with frustration involve the three elements of frustration: the objective, the method used to obtain the objective, and the aggression produced when prevented from obtaining the objective.

1. The Objective Much frustration comes from seeking unrealistic objectives. Being upset because someone pulls in front of you on the freeway, forcing you to slow down, implies the objective is to travel the entire trip without ever being impeded or slowed by anything. How realistic is that? Frustration is inevitable when the objective is unobtainable. People with impossibly high standards will never have self-esteem because they will never measure up to what they think they should be. Examine your objectives; if they are not realistic and obtainable, change them!

Many times, the objective is okay—what needs to be changed is your attitude toward it. Some well-intentioned people try to avoid frustration by eliminating all desire. They argue that if you don't want anything, you can't be frustrated in obtaining it. This is the method used by the Buddhist religion to obtain a state of supreme bliss and enlightenment known as Nirvana. Unfortunately, wanting to obtain Nirvana is a desire, and wanting to eliminate all desire is an objective. Frustration abounds!

If the ambition to have no ambition isn't your idea of happiness anyway, there is a more practical method for reducing frustration. Change your *expectations* to *preferences*.

2. The Method If the objective is realistic and obtainable but you still aren't having success in achieving it, change the method you are using to obtain your objective. If what you are doing doesn't work, don't butt your head against the wall; try something else.

3. The Aggression Aggression, usually identified as anger, isn't bad—it's just a source of energy. What you do with it is what determines if it's good or bad. Gasoline can be used to burn down your house and everything in it, including you. But it can also be used to power an automobile and provide you with better transportation. Understanding that anger is the most common reaction to frustration gives you the ability to plan and choose how you are going to use it. You can choose to use it as a source of energy to overcome obstacles or as another source of stress.

Conflict Conflict is the result of contradictory goals, or means, competing with each other and interfering with the smooth transition toward the objective.

A conflict exists when there are alternative actions for meeting the same need, or when competing motives vie for selection. Choosing between steak or prime rib illustrates the first condition where two alternatives meet the same need. Both are methods of meeting your need for food, but both sound good and you can only have one or the other. Making a lot of money by compromising your ethical values is an example of competing motives. The opportunity to satisfy your need for money by violating your ethical standards produces intense conflict for some people. In either case, the conflict involves the frustration of one need to meet another.

The concept of conflict embodies the assumption that the competing alternatives are of equal or almost equal importance. Also implicit in the definition of conflict is the requirement to make a decision. Conflict is resolved when a decision is made. However, since a decision entails the gain of one thing at the loss of another, indecision is the most frequent corollary to conflict. People in conflict procrastinate, vacillate, and agitate over the "right" decision to make.

There are three major types of conflict. The first is having to make a choice between two equally desirable goals. Like choosing between apple pie or chocolate cake (uh-uh, not fair taking both!). This may seem like the problem to have if you have to have a problem, but the conflict can become extremely distressing when a high value is placed on both alternatives. If achieving the pay raise you have longed for means moving from the home you love, the conflict can be agonizing.

The second is having to choose something that combines both good and bad qualities. Some people have that kind of conflict about marriage. The advantages of being single are compared with the disadvantages of marriage and vice versa. The conflict has created turmoil in many a hesitant bachelor. The conflict caused by deciding to get into a marriage is exceeded by the conflict many people feel about getting out of a marriage. Feeling trapped and unfulfilled in an empty, loveless marriage that is also financially secure has caused years of tortured indecision for some wives. Husbands have endured years of agony when the only thing holding them in the marriage was the dreadful thought of losing their children.

Another unfortunately common conflict is having to choose between the devil or the deep blue sea. This is the type of conflict in which neither one of the goals is desirable—such as going to the dentist or having a toothache—but you have to choose anyway. Either decision involves pain and you feel "damned if you do, and damned if you don't."

Dependency-independency conflicts, love-hate conflicts, sexual conflicts, and value conflicts are all common sources of stress. Each of them insists that the conflicted person choose a course of action. This demand to adjust in the face of opposing forces clamoring for attention can result in marked personality disturbance.

The most common reactions to conflict are anxiety and avoidance. Anxiety signals the potential danger associated with a decision, and avoidance is an attempt to deny or run away from the problem. This "running away," either literally or emotionally through fantasy, can lead to severe adjustment problems. Try some of the following ideas to reduce them.

> 1. Make a list of the decisions available to you in the conflict. Consider the example of a conflict about staying in a marriage. The choices are staying in the marriage or getting out of the marriage, so make two columns titled "Stay" and "Go." Then list all the possible advantages of each choice. You can adapt the method to your own conflict, but this example will give you a list of advantages under the column titled "Stay" and a list of advantages under the column titled "Go." Re-examine each list to make sure that the items accurately reflect all of your feelings. Now give each item a rating between one and ten to

reflect its importance to you. Total the scores and subtract the "Stay-Advantages" score from the "Go-Advantages" score. Decide in favor of the highest score.

2. Quit expecting to find the perfect decision. There are few, if any, perfect decisions. How you act after you make the decision is usually more important than the decision you make.

3. Quit expecting to have no doubts once you make a decision. By definition, conflicts are produced from opposing choices with equal or almost equal values, and doubts are inevitable.

4. Understand that in many instances the act of "making a decision" is more important than the decision you make.

5. Don't hesitate to seek outside help for crucial decisions about which you have conflict.

Pressure   Pressure is an adjustment demand that is created by having to speed up, intensify, or change the direction of goal-oriented behavior. It is most commonly represented by the feeling of "I should" or "I have to." As with frustration, pressure can be generated from within us or from our environment.

Some people have internalized standards which drive them mercilessly toward such high levels of attainment that they are kept under constant stress and strain. Regardless of their achievements, they will not permit themselves relief from self-imposed pressure.

Then there are pressures from the environment. The media have created a gigantic, ravenous beast called "the consumer." This animal is constantly being teased into a buying frenzy by advertisements that challenge it to look better, smell better, dress better, drive better, and live better. Personal standards may be sacrificed to feed this beast or, worse yet, never developed as the consumer adopts media standards as its own.

In this competitive, rapidly changing society, standards are constantly being elevated, and the pressure can be constant and unremitting if you try to keep up. The pressure to "keep up with the Joneses" can drive you insane. As one recently hospitalized patient told his therapist, "I got this breakdown from trying to keep up with my neighbors." "Yes, that can cause a lot of pressure," intoned the doctor. "Oh, that wasn't the problem," replied the patient. "I was doing fine, until. . . ." "Until what?" the therapist interrupted. "Until they refinanced!" sighed the patient.

With many sources of influence evaluating our conduct with scrupulous standards and idealistic regimens, it is easy to fall victim to pressuring yourself to meet expectations, even when they are unrealistic and destructive.

The most common reaction to the pressure of "shoulds" and "have to's" is resistance.

It has been said that the only things you *have* to do are to die and pay taxes. That's not true. The only thing you *have* to do is to die. Everything else is a choice. "But I'll go to jail if I don't pay taxes," you say. Yes, but you still don't *have* to pay them. You can choose not to, even if the choice is unwise.

All pressure is self-generated. You are the only one who creates it. Others can offer it to you but you have to accept it before it becomes pressure. The best method for dealing with pressure is to remember that pressure is a "tool" designed to help you accomplish a task. If the "tool" is helping you accomplish a task, then keep it. If the "tool" is harming you, reject it. You are its creator and it is your creature. If you don't like what you have created, get rid of it.

It's apparent to you that all three types of adjustment demands can occur at once. When you are feeling frustrated, in conflict, and under pressure all at the same time, that's real trouble. Your *stress* will rapidly become "distress" because you will be reacting with anger, anxiety, avoidance, and resistance.

The most serious adjustment demands are determined by their duration, importance, and multiplicity. The adjustment demands that are the most stressful are the ones requiring the greatest amount of change from our usual pattern of coping, involve our dearest values, last a long time, and contain all demand types — frustration, conflict, and pressure.

MEASURING YOUR STRESS

Drs. Holmes and Rahe have researched a list of typical adjustment demands to determine the degree of stress that each one creates. In their now well known Social Readjustment Rating Scale, they rated each adjustment demand from one (1) to one hundred (100). They called each rating point a Life Change Unit (LCU). The more serious an adjustment was, the more LCUs it was assigned.

When a person accumulated 300 LCUs in a given year, they had an eighty percent chance of developing a major mental or physical disorder in the next two years. As the number of LCUs increased, so did the potential for mental or physical illness.

I have drawn a real case history from my files, with identifying features removed, to illustrate how the concept of LCUs can be used to evaluate the severity of typical adjustment demands. I have described each adjustment demand experienced and listed its LCU rating.

Refer to the Social Readjustment Rating Scale on page 40 and follow along as the story of Steven R. unfolds. This is the type of story that happens every day and may even have happened, with some variation, to you.

Steve was an ambitious young business executive who sought therapy because he felt he was on the verge of a nervous breakdown. He was an intelligent, upwardly mobile young man who didn't have any readily apparent personality flaws. It rapidly became obvious that his current problem was acute in nature

SOCIAL READJUSTMENT RATING SCALE

Life Change Event	Life Change Units
Death of spouse	100
Divorce	73
Marital separation	65
Jail term	63
Death of close family member	63
Personal injury or illness	53
Marriage	50
Fired from work	47
Marital reconciliation	45
Retirement	45
Change in family member's health	44
Pregnancy	40
Sex difficulties	39
Addition to family	39
Business readjustment	39
Change in financial status	38
Death of close friend	37
Change to a different line of work	36
Change in number of marital arguments	35
Mortgage or loan over $10,000	31
Foreclosure of mortgage or loan	30
Change in work responsibilities	29
Son or daughter leaving home	29
Trouble with in-laws	29
Outstanding personal achievement	28
Spouse begins or stops work	26
Starting or finishing school	26
Change in living conditions	25
Revision of personal habits	24
Trouble with boss	23
Change in work hours or conditions	20
Change in residence	20
Change in schools	20
Change in recreational habits	19
Change in church activities	19
Change in social activities	18
Mortgage or loan under $10,000	17
Change in sleeping habits	16
Change in number of family gatherings	15
Change in eating habits	15
Vacation	13
Christmas season	12
Minor violation of the law	11

rather than the result of a disturbed development. He told me this story.

The previous year, he had taken a position with increased responsibility at a new company (Outstanding personal achievement = 28 LCUs, Change in responsibilities at work = 29 LCUs, Change in work hours = 20 LCUs).

His wife and he began to argue more as Steve's demanding schedule left her feeling deprived and neglected (Change in number of arguments with spouse = 35 LCUs). Steve angrily denounced her lack of understanding and support. Their sex life suffered (Sex difficulties = 39 LCUs).

In time, with growing unhappiness and discontent, they agreed to separate (Marital separation = 65 LCUs, then several Changes: residence = 20 LCUs, living conditions = 25 LCUs, personal habits = 24 LCUs, social activities = 18 LCUs, and number of family get-togethers = 15 LCUs).

Apart from each other, happier memories prevailed, and they decided to reconcile (Marital reconciliation = 45 LCUs — some days it just doesn't pay to get out of bed!). A few weeks after the reconciliation, they came to the bitter realization that nothing had changed. Each still felt deprived and unappreciated. So once more they separated, repeating the same number of LCUs as before. Eventually they divorced (Divorce = 73 LCUs).

Even though this is just a superficial synopsis of a real marital tragedy, the ingredients of a severe stress reaction are apparent. Steve was perplexed at his emotional fragility because he felt he was over the "worst part of it." He compounded his agitation by being angry at himself for not "snapping out of it."

While his wife was not my patient, she obviously had her own story and her own stress. But my concern was with my patient, Steve, and I found him a little stunned and somewhat sobered as he looked at a detailed list of what he had been through over the last year. His LCU total came to 585 LCUs in one year!

With that amount of stress, it was no wonder he felt on the verge of a nervous breakdown! Only being "on the verge" was a testimony to his personality integration under the circumstances. The number of stressful changes in his life was staggering, and that was merely counting the major ones.

I looked at him, and he looked at me. Both of us seemed to be waiting for him to self-destruct. "I guess I've been lucky," Steve said. "I'm in pretty good shape in comparison to what might be expected." "Yes," I agreed, "it is somewhat surprising that you haven't had anything worse than your mental agitation." "Well," he added, "I was in the hospital for a while with a bleeding ulcer. But that wasn't related to my divorce, . . . was it?"

This synopsis is a fairly typical scenario of a marital disintegration. Most people, like Steve, underestimate the stressful impact this type of event can have on their lives. Instead of taking the precautions their psychological and physical vulnerability mandate, they increase their potential for a health catastrophe by adding unnecessary stressors to their lives.

With stress compounded by the rate and amount of change in a period of time, you had better slow down when you are under a lot of stress. Don't add more change to adjust to . . . cool it! Yet many newly divorced or separated people decide that this is a good time to revamp their personalities. When what they need is time to emotionally reorganize, instead they go on crash diets, buy new wardrobes, sports cars, and otherwise increase their stress with unnecessary changes.

Adjustment demands need not be negative to be stressful. The deciding factor is whether or not the change requires a deviation from your usual pattern, and the amount of deviation required. Marriage, for instance, is worth 50 LCUs on the rating scale. Yet marriage is normally considered to be a positive event. Just ask anyone who has been married, however, and they will affirm that marriage entails some significant modifications to your lifestyle.

While the ratings on the Social Readjustment Rating Scale are valid in general, it's not accurate to say that every change will affect every person in the same way. Culture and personality both influence the magnitude of the specific stressful results of a given change.

There may also be some variance in the intensity of the stress experienced, based on the context in which the change occurs. A person marrying for the fifth time is unlikely to get as excited about it as a newlywed. An event to which one is accustomed requires fewer adjustments than one being experienced for the first time. As in the expression, "one man's meat is another man's poison," what may be a highly stressful vocational task for inexperienced Susan could be a routine operation for experienced Carol.

Understanding the stress potential of specific life events is part of the solution for coping with change. Dealing with change calls for stress-reducing techniques such as planning ahead how best to cope with anticipated change. Minimizing unnecessary changes during a time of stress is also obviously desirable. But much more than that is required. A more-detailed discussion of dealing with adjustment demands is covered in Chapter 8, but, before that, you need to understand the other side of the coin.

Chapter Four

Old Dogs and New Tricks

The second part of our Stress Formula, F + R = S, concerns the concept of "Resistance." While the term "Force" is defined as adjustment demands, it is represented by such things as pressure, frustration, and conflict. The concept "Resistance" in our formula refers to our reluctance to change from our usual pattern of coping. Some resistance to change is a normal and even necessary reaction, but the type and amount of resistance you have to change is a principal factor in determining your vulnerability to stress. There is an innate tendency to resist change known as psychological homeostasis. It is the progenitor of its less attractive offspring, stubbornness and hardheadedness.

You may be familiar with homeostasis in the biological sense. In biology, it pertains to the tendency of the organism to maintain its living systems within a range essential for survival. For example, your blood pressure must remain within a certain range. If it gets too high or too low, you may die.

Perhaps a more graphic example is how the body regulates its temperature. On an extremely hot day, your body temperature can soar and become life threatening. To guard against this kind of danger, a part of your brain, called the hypothalamus, sends out regulating messages to various parts of your body. One set of instructions causes the pores of your skin to enlarge, permitting dissipation of body heat. Sweat glands secrete their offerings and, as the perspiration evaporates, this temporarily cools the surface of the skin, reducing body heat.

First-time travelers to the Middle East are bewildered to see the desert nomads wearing long woolen robes. These solar experts have learned that they stay cooler in their torrid heat zone by perspiring copiously and letting it evaporate. The robes, called burnooses, facilitate this process. Unenlightened tourists frolic about in tank tops and bermuda shorts, falling victim to heat prostration.

The arteries, veins, and capillaries making up your circulation system are also involved in the homeostatic process. In hot weather, deep internal blood vessels constrict while vessels nearer to the surface dilate. This forces the blood to leave the deeper and hotter areas of the body and move to the surface, where it is cooler. Consequently, as the temperature climbs, your skin develops a predictable red, flushed appearance.

Another communication from the brain informs the large muscle groups to decrease their activity. Muscle contractions create heat through friction. Your body, not wishing any more heat, restricts movement through a characteristic hot-day lassitude and lethargy. However, there is an advantage to this phenomenon for the creatively lazy. The next time your spouse wishes you to perform some strenuous activity on a hot summer day, you can say, "Honey, personally I'd love to, but homeostasis just keeps saying, 'relax, and have a cold drink!'"

As you might expect, in cold weather the opposite reactions occur. Instead of your pores enlarging with an increase in perspiration, you perspire less and your pores close up tight to conserve body heat. In point of fact, your pores close up so tightly that the little muscles around the hair follicles "kink up" and form small bumps. We call them goose bumps or goose flesh.

Opposite reactions are also initiated in the circulatory system. Constriction and dilation of the blood vessels are reversed. The blood leaves the surface of the skin, pooling in the viscera, where it's warmer. As this ensues, your skin takes on the pale, clammy appearance associated with cold weather. Since the blood has also left the extremities, the fingers, toes, tip of the nose, and earlobes are the first places to become frostbitten.

Your energy level is affected because your body now desires the friction heat of muscle contraction. If you don't supply this movement via increased activity, your body will do it for you with involuntary contractions and spasms. We call this shivering.

PSYCHOLOGICAL HOMEOSTASIS

By now, you must be wondering what this basic biology discussion has to do with stress. The answer is, a great deal.

The fact of biological homeostasis is recognized, and it is understood as indispensable to good health. What is not as well known or understood, however, is that psychological homeostasis is just as natural and just as essential to health—the health of the personality—and the health of your personality centers around your self-esteem.

Self-esteem is to the personality what good health is to the body. When we have it, everything else works better. Good health helps prevent the body from becoming ill, and it facilitates the process of healing if the body does get sick. So it is with self-esteem. High self-esteem makes the personality resistant to mental illness, and it promotes a rapid recovery if the personality does get ill.

Damage to your self-esteem can cripple your personality as certainly as your body can be crippled. Feelings of unworthiness leave you vulnerable to many types of mental illnesses. And they seriously impair your ability to fulfill your potential. For that reason, threats to self-esteem are defended against by the personality as fervently as your body protects its health.

Psychological homeostasis is one of the methods your mind uses to guard against this threat. During the process of growing up, events occur which have the potential to damage the developing personality. Feelings of anxiety act as the burglar alarm of the personality. When a threat to self-esteem arises, anxiety signals the need to defend against it. In response, we adopt defense mechanisms intended to give *immediate* relief from the threat. Unfortunately, since the thrust of the defensive behavior is to provide immediate relief, the long-term consequences may not be positive. In this manner, personality characteristics may be acquired that, at the time, may temporarily defend against a self-esteem threat but are not to our ultimate advantage.

For instance, a patient of mine, George S., grew up in an atmosphere of abusive criticism. The criticism was so pervasive and destructive that accepting it as valid would irreparably damage his personality. To defend against this possibility, he adopted the defense mechanism called denial. Now all incoming criticism was sidestepped by merely ignoring or rejecting it as invalid. That was fine as a child when the criticism was harsh and unconstructive, but continuing to use denial as an adult caused George more problems than it solved.

George simply could not, or would not, admit when he was wrong. Aside from the misery it caused to those who loved him, consider the paralysis it caused George. By never acknowledging when he was wrong, he was denied the opportunity to learn from his experiences. He couldn't profit from instruction and therefore couldn't grow as a person. It got so bad that even the implication of criticism would cause him to react with indignant defensiveness.

Since the respect of his family was paramount to George, the denial was at its worst with them. He couldn't apologize, ask forgiveness, express sorrow, or do any of the humanizing things that make relationships viable. He couldn't improve as a husband or father because of the implicit suggestion of error. He was truly paralyzed. Poor wife, poor family, poor George.

Now there is nothing wrong with the need to defend your ego. However, as in the case of George, two problems that can inhibit the healthy development of your personality commonly transpire. The first is when you become defensive to a perceived threat that is, in fact, minimal or non-existent. This creates an oversensitivity that can cause you to act defensively in non-threatening situations. The second is when defensive behaviors that may have been appropriate in one setting are used in a new situation where they are inappropriate. This is illustrated by George's inability to accept constructive criticism, and his instinctive reaction of denying any fault just as if it were the destructive abuse of his past.

Both of these reactions prevent the growth and expansion of the personality by curtailing the opportunity for new and corrective experiences. Also, by limiting adaptive flexibility, they exacerbate stress.

Once a set of defense mechanisms becomes absorbed as part of our personality, it is then "locked in" by psychological homeostasis. In reference to the difficulty we have in changing as we get older, there is a popular adage, "you can't teach an old dog new tricks." There is indeed much truth to the idea that we get more resistant to change as we get older. When we learn a relatively effective coping style, we tend to repeat it with an ever-increasing resistance to change. Then, when life circumstances require us to adapt and we lack the motivation or the skills, the result is stress.

Consider a patient of mine who grew up in an atmosphere of humiliation and "put-downs." He learned to see the world as a threatening place and developed an inordinate fear of social ridicule and rejection. To avoid the anticipated humiliation and rejection of social involvement, he adopted withdrawal as a means of self-protection. Despite a longing to relate and be an active participant in social life, he became touchy, evasive, and mistrustful. He gravitated to the field of engineering where his skill with "things" was valued and social skills were not required.

By avoiding people as much as possible, he was able to reduce anxiety and maintain his psychological equilibrium. But, when he was pressed into a situation where he could not avoid people, such as when his employer required him to make a speech at a business meeting, he was overwhelmed with anxiety. But soon the skill and knowledge he displayed in his profession captured the attention of his superiors who promoted him into a management position. That did it. Now he was subjected daily to the awareness of his social deficits as his detached management style provoked criticism from his subordinates. Raised to his "level of incompetence," robbed of the self-esteem his previous competence provided, and trapped between complaining subordinates and superiors, he rapidly acquired "distressing" physical and psychological symptoms.

The "Force," in this situation, was the implicit demand for him to change his coping style of withdrawing; and the "Resistance" was his inability and unwillingness to do so. The result was a debilitating stress reaction. The intensity of the stress was in direct proportion to increases in "Force," or demands to change, and "Resistance," or his unwillingness to change.

Another case was very similar to this. Bill S. came to see me by reference of his family physician. He had been complaining of chest pains, headaches, difficulty in sleeping, and increasing irritability. Bill confessed to me privately that he had also been drinking more than usual. He felt he needed it to relax. In reviewing Bill's recent history, he revealed that he had made a major career change within the last few months. He had taken a supervisory position with an electronics firm, following retirement from the military.

Bill was very industrious and efficient, with a no-nonsense attitude toward his work. Productivity, working hard, and getting the job done were his priorities, with people concerns being of minimal importance. These attitudes were quite functional in the military and even earned him praise and recognition.

But that wasn't true in his current position. The workers he supervised had poor morale and low effectiveness. Furthermore, they had begun to complain to Bill's boss. They said he was often tactless and abrupt, and too direct and gruff. Some of the complainers accused him of "talking down to them," being impatient, and having a "swelled head." It became obvious that Bill's symptoms were stress-related. His unwillingness and inability to adapt to his new situation by learning a more effective management style was the primary cause.

The case of Bill S. is another example of how the stress formula operates. In his circumstances, the "Force" was represented by his subordinates' ineffectiveness and low morale. Their complaints about Bill made the implicit demand, "Do something else, Bill; what you're doing doesn't work." The "Resistance" part of the formula is illustrated by Bill's refusal to recognize that his management style was creating the problem. Bill felt the only solution to the problem was to fire the employees. "After all," said Bill, "it's not my fault that they are lazy and incompetent."

By insisting on being harsh and abrasive with his subordinates because it seemed to be effective in a previous work setting, Bill was ignoring the reality that the situation had changed. He was, in effect, making the demand that the situation adjust to him instead of making the adjustment himself.

As you learn about the role of resistance in the production of stress, you may have a question: how do some of the exceptionally rigid people you have met survive? The answer is twofold. They either gravitate to situations where adjustment is not required, or they surround themselves with people who are willing to make the constant adjustments necessary to live with them. When they cannot find such a situation, or those around them are no longer willing to put up with their obnoxious behavior, their emotional fragility becomes apparent.

And so it was with Bill. He had created a protected world for himself both at home and on the job. He had picked a passive woman to marry because she accepted his brusque, intimidating manner as strength. Later on in the marriage, whenever her needs were jeopardized by his behavior, he could always over-power her complaints and put her on the defensive with a blus-tering, debasing counterattack.

His job in the military was similarly protected from any serious challenge to his adequacy. Bill was buffered from threat by an unusual and psychologically safe "ecological niche" that he had unconsciously created himself. Supported by a wife who either never challenged him or always lost when she did, kids who were easily controlled by intimidation, friends who shared his aggres-sive attitudes, and a job where his belligerence was rewarded, Bill had little incentive to examine his actions. He barreled through life, trailing victims in his wake, convinced that his way was the right way, and feeling fine.

But now things were different!

Bill had made a major change in his life. He had left the unique situation of the military where his pugnacious manner seemed to be effective, and had moved to a new setting where it didn't work. For the first time, he was faced with the ineffective-ness of his conduct. When facing criticism, his previously suc-cessful techniques of becoming more aggressive and intimidating now only made matters worse. Bill was finding out that not only was his behavior not appreciated but he could actually lose his job because of it. He was confused and angry.

It didn't have to be that way. Bill could have minimized the stress of this major change in his life by doing two things.

First, he needed to simply recognize that some change in him might be necessary and plan for it. In general, it's a good idea to regularly reassess our coping styles and make needed modifi-cations. One method of doing this is to have honest talks with trusted friends and associates. Listening to people who love you can provide valuable insight.

Periodic "checkups" with a counselor or therapist can be an important addition to your annual physical. It is ironic that the same person who gets an annual physical even though he feels fine, and who regularly "tunes up" his car even though it runs adequately, would never think of seeing a therapist—unless he were forced to by mental illness or outside pressure.

You may think me crazy, if you don't already, but there is another source of input you ought to consider. When appraising your coping style for needed modification, don't forget to listen to your enemies. That's right, listen to your enemies! This may be the most distasteful way to hear what you need to hear, but it may also be the most effective. Your enemies—those people who don't care about you at all or who normally care but are temporarily mad at you—may be the only ones with enough emotional distance and disregard for tact to tell you the truth!

Oh, they won't say it as you would prefer to hear it. They'll probably couch it in objectionable language and try to shove it down your throat. But try listening to the substance of it. Strip it of all the nasty verbiage and ask yourself the magic question: Is it true?

If you do that, you may just hear the thing you most need to hear. Your enemies may have unwittingly done you an immense favor with their criticism. Instead of harming you, it could very well enhance the quality of your life.

But Bill did none of these things. While making plans to deal with the effects of this change on him financially, he saw no need to plan for its effects on him personally.

The second thing Bill could have done to minimize stress is obvious. After assessing the need for change and finding it desirable, he could have changed! Adaptation is the keystone of successful evolution. Adapting to his new environment by learning effective management skills would have helped Bill evolve into a more successful manager and a better person.

Bill didn't do that either, of course. Old coping patterns die hard, and Bill found it easier to declare the company "all screwed up" and quit his job. He found another job where he eventually became known as a hard worker who just couldn't manage people. The last thing I heard was that Bill's dead-end second career had left him a bitter man who drank too much and talked about the great days when he was in the Army.

Now that we have briefly examined the concepts of Force and Resistance as they relate to stress, let's plug them back into The Stress Formula. When the circumstances of life demand that you adapt to a new situation (Force), and you resist the change in preference to your old coping style (Resistance), you will experience Stress. The best definition of stress may very well be: *the wear and tear on a person that comes from dealing with life.* The more skillful you are at adapting, the longer it will take for you to wear out. People with narrow and limited coping patterns are psychologically vulnerable people and the first to succumb to stress in a changing environment.

I have found that those who handle stress the best tend to view life as a huge classroom. Instead of fighting change, they use it to learn more about themselves. They have the flexibility to assimilate change and use it as fuel for growth and development.

In general, being resistant to change increases stress. But, on the other hand, it isn't always wise to blindly adapt to every change. In our original illustration of The Stress Formula, resistance was likened to the resistance of steel girders in a bridge to the impact of traffic crossing it. If the steel girders didn't resist the traffic to some degree, they couldn't handle the impact at all. If they completely caved in to the pressure, there would be no stress, but there wouldn't be a bridge either!

Steel resists force but it also has the ability to give a little. If it didn't, it would break. There must be some resistance to change in your coping strategies, but it must not become rigidity. Having enough resistance to change so that you are a thinking person with convictions, but stopping short of being unreasonably stubborn, is the task.

Can you tell the difference between resistance and rigidity? The easy answer is to ascribe your behavior to honorable motives and someone else's to negative personality traits. For example, when it's you, it's perseverance; when it's someone else, it's stubbornness. When it's you, it's conviction; when it's someone else, it's narrow-mindedness. That may be easy, but not helpful. The distinction between healthy resistance and unhealthy rigidity is not that simple, and you need to know the difference. It is a crucial distinction to be able to make when you are coping with stress.

Chapter Five

Is Charlie Castiron Really Strong?

All of this emphasis on adaptability is not intended to suggest that resistance is bad. Our resistance to change is not innately unhealthy. Imagine how difficult life would be if we had to "start from scratch" every time we faced a new situation. Our ability to learn the skill sequences required in routine situations produces an efficiency of effort needed for effective living.

Consider how much time would be wasted if we had to relearn to tie our shoes or put on our clothes every day. We engage in hundreds of behaviors daily that involve skills which we have learned and filed away in our mental computer. As life situations activate the expression of these skills, they are exhibited with minimal thought from us about "how to do it."

Every person has a reservoir of such coping skills that range from the simple — e.g., picking up a fork — to the complex, such as socializing at a party. These behaviors become the core behaviors of what we know as personality. They are almost reflexive in their expression, requiring little or no forethought.

When you tie your shoe, your mind is capable of thinking of other things while your hands perform their almost automatic movements. From tying our shoes to shaving or putting on makeup, we seldom deviate from our established procedures for these daily routines.

It's easy to see how valuable this can be. By having some behaviors virtually automated, time and energy are freed to be expended on more important issues.

But what if the behaviors aren't efficient? What if someone was taught that the way to tie shoes was with one hand? Even if they had become fairly adept at doing this, it would still not be the most efficient method of tying one's shoes. The problem is that, once a behavior is learned, whether or not it is efficient and desirable, it is added to our repertoire and becomes resistant to change. While this frees up attention and energy for other tasks, it also protects inefficient or partially effective behaviors from modification.

None of this is particularly significant until we realize that cognitions are a form of behavior. Our cognitions, or thoughts, can become as automated as our actions.

We have all met individuals who seem to have "knee-jerk" responses to words, situations, or people. It is as if a "button" is pushed and the behavior that follows is like a reflex. If you know a person's "buttons," you can play them like an instrument, orchestrating their conduct by pushing their "buttons" and producing the automatic behavior. The sight of a black face, for some people, can trigger a set of thoughts that are engaged in as reflexively as the actions involved in tying one's shoe. The way some people react to situations or people is as if their credo is, "My mind is made up; don't confuse me with the facts."

As indicated, these automatic thoughts and actions, or "buttons," can be beneficial if they are appropriate, realistic responses. But that's not always the case. I once knew a woman whose house caught fire. While running out of the raging inferno, she stopped to turn off the lights and lock the door. Similarly, our response to stressors can be as automatic in its effect and just as endangering.

But, in spite of this, resistance to change isn't always bad. It can help us endure troublesome predicaments by providing a degree of stability. If we were blown about by every wind of change that came our way, we would find it impossible to live successfully. Psychological homeostasis permits us to be more efficient in our responses to situations, through compiling a storehouse of competencies from which we can draw.

You may have experienced times when the pressure to change was intense, but you held firm and it worked out to your advantage. People who do this may even be described as having integrity, or strong moral character. That's all well and good when your coping responses are rational, appropriate, and variable enough to allow you to adapt to changing circumstances.

Problems occur when the responses are irrational, inappropriate, and limited. When that occurs, instead of your behavior being described as determined and persistent, it will probably be called stubborn and hardheaded. Rather than showing moral character, it demonstrates narrow-mindedness.

There are conditions when you should adapt, and situations where you should stand firm. To paraphrase St. Francis, the art of living requires that "we adapt when we need to adapt, stand firm when we need to stand firm, and have the wisdom to know the difference."

Just as biological homeostasis strives to keep our physical systems within a range necessary to the integrity of the body, psychological homeostasis strives to minimize changes in our response to the environment to protect the integrity of the personality. But this innate efficiency expert, operating to prevent us from always reinventing the wheel, must not be permitted to exist without examination.

All of our behaviors need periodic re-examination and evaluation. That brings us to the second strategy for stress.

Stress Strategy #2

Don't resist change blindly.
Develop the flexibility to adapt.

An essential factor of effective stress management is that our resistance to change must not be so intense and unexamined that we are unable to adapt to changing circumstances.

Although inflexibility accentuates stress, many people associate it with strength. They view their rigid, uncompromising behavior as a virtue. They tend to dominate and control. They run roughshod over the feelings and opinions of others, insisting on being seen as right in every situation. For them, admitting that they are wrong is like confessing to a crime. They may have a lot of faults, but being wrong isn't one of them! They form opinions quickly and defend them vociferously. Those who fail to agree with them are viewed with contempt and dismissed as stupid or ignorant.

In spite of this rather unattractive picture, they usually admire themselves for their "strength." While willing to acknowledge that they may be hard-boiled and blunt, they prefer to describe themselves as honest, direct, and realistic. People who can't handle them are considered weak and not to be taken seriously.

They believe that their snap judgments reflect decisiveness, and that their refusal to seriously evaluate new, potentially contradictory information demonstrates conviction. They gain support from the fact that there are people who share their beliefs. This provides a mutual admiration society which serves to strengthen their rigidity and self-righteousness.

"CHARLIE CASTIRON" AND FRIENDS

There is a parallel to this concept of strength in the science of metallurgy. Metallurgy is the discipline that examines the qualities and properties of metal. In this field, there are two well-analyzed metals, both valued for their strength. One of these metals, cast iron, is remarkably similar to the kind of strength that is derived from personality rigidity. To examine the similarities, let's create a hypothetical person called "Charlie Castiron."

Like cast iron, Charlie has admirable qualities of strength. He can withstand a lot of pressure, he can be pounded on with no noticeable effect, and he never bends. But also like cast iron, his strength is one-dimensional. He can endure pressure only as long as you don't require him to change his form. If the forces assailing him demand a change in his form, he will break!

Over the years, Charlie has acquired a set of beliefs, attitudes, and behaviors that is now set in concrete. In his mind, he's pretty sure he has a handle on the way things really are, and he considers everyone out of step except himself and the ones who agree with him.

Unwilling to change, and seeing no need to anyway, Charlie organizes his life so that the only adjustments necessary are from those with whom he associates. Charlie's absolute certainty of the correctness of his behavior and beliefs frequently draws the admiration of those who are certain of nothing. They flock to him as a paragon of strength, and their admiration reinforces his certainty. The combination of Charlie's assuredness and his sarcastic disparagement of opposing viewpoints is very convincing. Those he can't convince, he intimidates. Those he can't convince or intimidate, he contemptuously dismisses as stupid.

Charlie has carefully created a protected environment. And in this environment, he is indeed the master. Charlie has circumscribed his world so that it contains no ambiguity or uncertainty. It is a small world in which every problem has an answer. Leaving nothing to chance, Charlie makes sure every issue in his life conforms to the way he thinks. Seeing all problems as black and white makes it easy for Charlie to apply his black and white values. Not having to deal with ambiguity or uncertainty frees Charlie from having to think, be creative, or adapt, and he looks strong and confident.

In the presence of stress, Charlie becomes even more rigid. This characteristic frequently leads to others perceiving him as "a rock." "You can really count on ol' Charlie," they declare, and it's true that you can. Charlie is predictable and dependable—sometimes perversely so. His ability to reduce the world to the two dimensions of black and white gives Charlie the illusion of mastery and competence. Yes, Charlie has strength, but it's a brittle strength and maintained at great cost.

In spite of Charlie's apparent strength, he is peculiarly vulnerable to certain stresses. Charlie's "strength" is maintained by reducing the world to a kindergarten level in which simplistic coping skills suffice. His weakness is his inability to deal with a complex world requiring multidimensional coping skills.

In our rapidly developing, technology-dependent society, change is the rule—not the exception. We are under constant pressure to adjust and adapt to the almost-incessant demands of our constantly changing world. Historically valued principles are commonly challenged and frequently discarded. Many old values become irrelevant, and even some of the best of them may need updating and expansion. This produces severe stress in people who cannot, or refuse to, adapt. It also serves to minimize their personal growth.

In China, for several centuries, it was the custom in the higher class of Chinese society to bind the feet of female infants. Normally developed feet were considered unsightly and repulsive, tolerable only in the peasant class; and so infant girls' feet were tightly bound. This rigid, cast-like binding, repeated throughout early physical development, had the desired effect. The upper-class Chinese girl had very small feet—at the expense of being permanently crippled.

Charlie Castiron pays a similar price for his rigidly bound personality. Normal growth is curtailed and distorted, and Charlie becomes a caricature of strength.

The constant effort of trying to maintain his rigid posture in the face of the winds of change takes its toll on Charlie. His most vulnerable spot is his body. While it's true that he seldom has emotional breakdowns, his increased tendency for physical breakdowns reflects the high cost of his inner tension. His heightened susceptibility to heart failure is one aspect of the expense.

Charlie Castiron may appear admirably strong, but he can perpetuate that illusion only by creating a microcosm in which he rules. Exposed to the real world, Charlie's defenses crumble. It is then that his conviction begins to look like rigidity, his strength a cover-up for weakness, and his "leadership" is revealed as a need for control and domination.

And then there's "Peggy Plastic." Peggy Plastic isn't concerned with looking strong. She just wants to get along. The price she is willing to pay for acceptance is the surrender of her personhood. Accommodating, submissive, and malleable to a fault, she adopts the values of whichever authority seems most likely to accept and take care of her.

Although Peggy, in fact, may be an attractive and capable person, she has deep-seated feelings of inadequacy and worthlessness. She's certain that she can never cope with life all by herself. Doubting her worth, she feels that the only way she can attract someone to take care of her is by being especially helpful and kind. By not burdening anyone with her needs, and by always being alert to theirs, she is hopeful that someone will find her of value. Fearful of the rejection that asserting herself threatens, and unsure of her worth, she submerges her individuality in the service of her needs for approval and acceptance.

Since Peggy seeks security and protection, she is drawn to those who exude strength and confidence. So guess who she marries? That's right. And Peggy is the perfect foil for Charlie. At their best, she provides the unquestioning admiration and obedience he requires, and he offers her the protection and security she craves.

Charlie appears to be the strong one in this marriage, and he works hard to protect that image. Peggy discounts her own strength, but feels safe in the reflected confidence of her protector. When she is deprived of this guardianship through abandonment or disillusionment, she becomes acutely aware of her vulnerability. But Peggy has strength she doesn't even know exists. She's only aware of her tender, vulnerable, inadequate feelings, and there is much more to her than that. Since she has spent most of her life adjusting to the needs of others, she has become an expert at adaptability. If she can resist the impulse to run to another "protector," she will discover that she is surprisingly resilient.

The dinosaur was a strong, powerful animal, but it couldn't adapt to its changing environment. The dinosaur's great size and strength must have been quite impressive, but it wasn't enough. Whatever happened to these big, imposing animals? That's right. They became extinct. No matter how large, strong, or impressive they were, their inability to adjust their rigid lifestyle caused their downfall. Most of the frightened, vulnerable little animals of that time are still around in one form or another—but the dinosaur is gone.

It's a lot easier for an overly adaptable person to become strong than it is for a rigid person to develop flexibility.

Charlie Castiron feels good about himself but is inflexible. Peggy Plastic is very adaptable but lacks self-esteem. The best combination of the two is found in the qualities of another metal.

"Susan Steel" exemplifies the ideal balance between strength and vulnerability. Like her namesake, she can adjust and adapt to handle pressure from diverse directions without breaking. When necessary, she remains firm in the presence of adversity, absorbing the force without yielding to its influence. In situations where new information warrants intelligent change, she bends to the new direction and once again becomes stable. She is firm but not unbending, flexible but not flimsy. The ability to adapt to change is an invaluable tool for dealing with stress.

HOW FLEXIBLE ARE YOU?

You may be wondering just how flexible you really are. To stimulate your thoughts on the question of flexibility, fill out the following questionnaire. It's short and simple—no tricks—and the questions are exactly what they seem to be. Even though it is short and simple, I believe you'll find that it accomplishes its purpose which is to get you to think about how flexible you really are. The questionnaire is divided into two parts. To get the best results, answer Part 1 without looking at Part 2.

PART 1

1. Do you like cats?   Yes ___ No ___ Uncertain ___
2. Do you like raw oysters?   Yes ___ No ___ Uncertain ___
3. Would you like to live
   in Europe?   Yes ___ No ___ Uncertain ___
4. Do you like classical music?   Yes ___ No ___ Uncertain ___
5. Do you like to waltz?   Yes ___ No ___ Uncertain ___
6. Do you like lawyers?   Yes ___ No ___ Uncertain ___
7. Do you like East Indian
   food?   Yes ___ No ___ Uncertain ___
8. Do you like Rolls Royce
   cars?   Yes ___ No ___ Uncertain ___
9. Would you like to live
   in Tahiti?   Yes ___ No ___ Uncertain ___
10. Do you like square dancing?   Yes ___ No ___ Uncertain ___

Continue with Part 2 of this questionnaire and then we'll talk about what it means. Without referring to your previous answers, provide answers to the following questions. This time, the answers must be either yes or no. You may no longer be uncertain.

PART 2

1. Have you ever owned a cat for
   more than a month?   Yes __ No __
   (It had to be *your* cat!)
2. Have you ever eaten raw oysters?   Yes __ No __
   (Halfway doesn't count!)
3. Have you ever been to Europe?   Yes __ No __
4. Have you ever attended a symphony or listened
   to a complete recording of one?   Yes __ No __
5. Do you know how to waltz?   Yes __ No __
6. Have you ever used a lawyer
   or known one personally?   Yes __ No __
7. Have you ever eaten East Indian food?   Yes __ No __
8. Have you ever owned or driven
   a Rolls Royce?   Yes __ No __
9. Have you ever been to Tahiti?   Yes __ No __
10. Do you know how to square dance?   Yes __ No __

Now that you have finished the questionnaire, you're ready for
the fun part. You've heard of the term I.Q., right? Well, this
little test measures your F.Q. — your Flexibility Quotient. For each
set (Parts 1 & 2) of your answers, apply the following rules until
you find the one that matches.

	Part 1	**Part 2**	**Points**
Rule #1.	Yes or No	No	0
Rule #2.	Yes or No	Yes	1
Rule #3.	Uncertain	No	2
Rule #4.	Uncertain	Yes	3

To illustrate how the scoring works, let's use the first question as
an example.

> *Rule #1:* If to the first question on Part 1, "Do
> you like cats?" you answered either Yes or No,

and to the first question on Part 2, "Have you ever owned a cat for more than a month?" you answered No, that corresponds to Rule #1 and the score for that type of response is zero.

Rule #2: If, in Part 1, you answered Yes or No to question #1 "Do you like cats?" and in Part 2, question #1 you answered Yes, that corresponds to Rule #2, and the score for that type of response is 1.

Rule #3: If you answered Uncertain on Part 1, question #1, "Do you like cats?" and answered No on Part 2, question #1, that corresponds to Rule #3; give yourself 2 points for all responses matching that rule.

Rule #4: If you answered Uncertain to the question, "Do you like cats?" on Part 1; and on Part 2, question #1 you answered Yes, that corresponds to Rule #4; give yourself 3 points for all responses matching that rule.

Follow that procedure and give yourself a score for each set of questions. When you have completed this, total your points.

As you can see, the point totals range from 0 to 15. The average score for adult males is 10 points. Women average slightly higher than men at 11 points. Higher scores are associated with greater flexibility and tolerance, and lower scores with rigidity and intolerance.

Before we discuss the scores in more detail, remember this fact. Your score, whatever it is, is not statistically valid. So if you didn't like your score, don't get an ulcer wanting to dispute the questions with me. You're absolutely right that the test has a lot of holes in it. This exercise has one purpose, and one purpose only. That purpose is to get you to think about the way you form opinions.

Having said that, let's examine each scoring rule and analyze why the points are allotted as they are.

> *RULE #1:* For each set of answers that
> corresponds to this pattern, the score is zero.

If you think about it, the reasoning will be clear. The people with this response pattern are saying that they have made up their minds about the subject when they have never had any experience with it. The tendency to come to a conclusion about something without having any experience with it is characteristic of Charlie Castiron. It's one of the reasons he's so vulnerable to stress.

A friend of mine came to see me, greatly distressed that his daughter had decided to marry a member of a minority group. He was fussing and fuming so much about how this would destroy his daughter's life, not to mention the damage to the family reputation, that his wife feared he would have a heart attack.

It turned out that he had never even met his daughter's fiancé nor had he known anyone of that ethnic group. His attitude was created by assumptions he had held for years and had never bothered to critically evaluate.

I recommended that before he inflict any more emotional damage upon his family and physical damage to himself, he at least get to know the man personally. I pointed out that he wouldn't even make a decision to buy, or not buy, a car with the same amount of limited knowledge. He agreed, to his credit, and determined to get to know the person before he made a decision.

They got married (they would have anyway), and now he boasts to anyone who will listen about his great son-in-law. If he had remained rigid about his opinion, he would not only have missed knowing a fine person, and lost his daughter and grand-children, but he would have lived in a state of stress that could have shortened his life.

> *RULE #2:* For each set of answers that
> corresponds to this pattern, the score is 1.

This set of answers indicates that you have formed an opinion about the issue based on experience with it. It obviously makes more sense to reserve judgment on something until you have some experience with it. You can't evaluate the worthiness of anything without knowing something about it and, for this reason, this response pattern gets one point.

> *RULE #3:* For each set of answers that corresponds to this pattern, the score is 2.

This response indicates that the person has not come to a decision on the subject because of never having any experience with it. Clearly, there is a greater degree of objectivity in this response and therefore more points are warranted.

> *RULE #4:* For each set of answers that corresponds to this pattern, the score is 3.

This is an apparent absurdity. The maximum point total is given to people who haven't reached a decision about something even though they have had experience with it. At first glance, this would appear to be rewarding people for being wishy-washy and indecisive; but withhold judgment for a moment. Let's analyze why 3 points are given, using the first question as an example.

If the person doesn't know if he likes cats, even though he has owned one for more than a month, what could that mean? His response indicates that he will not make a judgment from one experience. While he may, or may not, have liked the cat he owned, he has not jumped to the conclusion that he likes or dislikes *all* cats.

Remember, as a kid, how one or two bad experiences could "sour" you on something; then later, as an adult, you found out you actually liked what you hated as a kid? For instance, I used to hate zucchini and now I love it. It frequently takes more than limited experience with something to make a proper evaluation. So this rule is rewarding those who withhold judgment until they have ample experience.

With that explanation, it might appear that the ideally open-minded person doesn't form an opinion on anything until he or she has sampled everything. And what about cancer? Do you have to experience cancer before you can say you don't like it? No, of course not. Neither one of these extremes is what open-mindedness is all about. To form opinions with no experience or evidence or to never have an opinion because of not being able to sample everything are both dangerous. Peggy Plastic hates to express an opinion about anything because she fears offending someone. That doesn't make her open-minded.

Somewhere between having no experience with something and knowing everything there is to know about it is the place to form an opinion. In general, the more important the issue, the longer you should reserve judgment. Unexamined opinions may not be important when it comes to cats, but just substitute the name of any ethnic group and you can see the wider implications.

Rigid people tend to form opinions quickly and seldom change them, even if there is contradictory evidence suggesting they are in error. Changing their opinion is like an admission of error, which they find abhorrent, or revealing a deficiency, which is equally abhorrent. They view changing their opinion as a weakness when, in fact, the inability to do so is the weakness.

If your score is 8 or below, you may tend toward narrow-mindedness and dogmatism. It may be that your decisions are based on emotion and you have difficulty changing your mind. Aside from the interpersonal and other problems this creates, it leaves you vulnerable to stress, and you have an elevated potential for heart attacks, ulcers, and other diseases of adaptation.

Scores between 9 and 11 fall into the mid-range which means your rigidity-tolerance levels are about the same as those of most people. Unfortunately, most people tend to be too rigid. A little more tolerance wouldn't hurt.

Scores of 12 or above would imply greater tolerance and open-mindedness. You may be more receptive to new experience and find it easier for your attitude to grow and change with your personality. You are less threatened by change, and welcome new information that expands your understanding of the world.

Now that you're either pleased with yourself or defensive and angry, may I remind you of what I said earlier. The scores have no statistical validity! They are meaningless. Unless you give them meaning — by thinking.

The purpose of the questionnaire is not to give you a score, a label, or put you in a category. The purpose is to stimulate you to reflect on the process you use to make decisions.

Do you make decisions based on emotion, or narrow and limited experience? Do you seek new and more comprehensive information with which to evaluate your opinions? Do you analyze your opinions from different perspectives and viewpoints to assess their validity?

There is nothing wrong with being convinced that your beliefs and attitudes are correct. In many cases, it may even be a virtuous characteristic. But understand that there is a difference between having convictions and being rigid. Rigid people never examine their beliefs; they just "know what they know."

Flexible people are aware of the need to subject important issues to objective scrutiny. They know that additional information can not only cause them to modify their opinions but can also amplify and strengthen them. Rigid people are "Uptight," flexible people are "All Right."

If this provocative little questionnaire has helped you to contemplate the method you use to form opinions about important issues in your life, then it has served its purpose. To successfully handle stress, you must be able to analyze situations honestly, and adapt to them as necessary. You must candidly evaluate your opinions in the light of new evidence, and change them where warranted.

Granted, this is a difficult task to perform with objectivity. But if you succeed, you will not only increase your stress resistance, you will permit your personality to breathe and expand. Trading mental rigidity for stress resistance, and stagnation for growth, is an offer you can't refuse. The alternative can be deadly.

Chapter Six

The Wages of Stress

There is a world of human experience represented by the Alarm, Resistance, and Exhaustion phases of the General Adaptation Syndrome. Those words, innocuous as they may seem, are measured in suffering and pain. The fact is that we pay a price when we deal with stressful situations. But we don't always realize that we're paying it.

When you have a full-blown stress reaction, it is obvious that something is seriously wrong. But stress doesn't usually hit us like an atomic bomb. Stressors usually come in bunches, not one at a time. At any given time, you may be sure you are handling the stress. But it tends to be cumulative in its effect. It sneaks up on us so that, in the early stages, we may not be aware that we are moving from stress to distress. Understanding some of the early warning signals is a valuable part of any stress-coping strategy. That concept is the third strategy for stress.

Stress Strategy #3

*Learn to recognize
the early warning signals of burnout
and take immediate action.*

COPING BURNOUT

Everyone has some ability to cope. Without it, we couldn't survive for very long. But just as skill levels vary in other activities, they also vary when it comes to coping. A third-year piano student and Vladimir Horowitz can both play the piano. But there is a vast difference in performance.

Here's a hypothetical example of two totally different types of coping—in the same person. The saga of Barney Burnout.

Barney was having a difficult day. Nothing had gone right at work for the last few weeks, and now this. He had arrived at the office expecting to collaborate with an associate on a crucial task, only to discover that his colleague was sick in bed. That left Barney with the responsibility of meeting the deadline and he was already swamped. "When it rains, it pours," Barney muttered to himself. "How can I drain the swamp when I'm up to my ears in alligators?"

As the day wore on, Barney's coping ability steadily deteriorated. He was certain his usually efficient secretary was deliberately trying to sabotage him. Unnecessary errors and delays were adding pressure and frustration. Barney's boss, while checking on the progress of his priority task, seemed to infer that Barney was deficient in his efforts. To top it off, the scuttlebutt around the coffee machine was that third-quarter earnings were down and there could be some layoffs.

Traffic was worse than usual on his commute home and, when he finally arrived, late, he was fuming. Blocked from pulling into the driveway by his youngest son's tricycle, Barney felt ready to explode. After throwing the trike into the yard and parking the car, Barney stormed toward the house. The young owner of the stray tricycle came running to meet his Dad but pulled up short as Barney began to rage. "I've told you a thousand times to put your things away when you're finished playing with them. If I see that tricycle in the driveway one more time when I get home, it's going to Goodwill!"

Barney's tirade continued as he found his other two children watching television in the family room. "Don't you kids have anything better to do than watch TV? How about your homework, or is that too much to ask?"

Anxious to placate her choleric husband, Barney's wife offered: "Honey, dinner's a little late but I'll have it ready in a jiffy. Can I get you a drink while you're waiting?" Barney erupted again. "Dinner's late again? Do you mean to tell me that you can't have a little thing like dinner ready on time? What do you think would happen at work if I didn't get things done on time? I work and slave to support this family and this is the thanks I get. . . . Of course I'll have a drink; it should have been obvious!" Stalking off to his study, leaving his confused and resentful family behind, Barney was heard to mutter, "I can't help it, I've had a hard day!"

Now Barney is basically a decent man who loves his family. If anyone else talked to his family that way, he would be furious. What turned him into a monster? According to Barney, it was because he "had a hard day." Well maybe Barney's day was a tough one at that; but let's take a look at the other side of the coin and explore this further.

Consider the difference it would make if, instead of things getting worse at work the last few weeks, they were getting better. What if Barney's day went like this?

Barney's boss openly commended him at a staff meeting for finishing that crucial assignment in spite of the lack of assistance. Privately, his boss intimated that the company had their eye on him and he could be in for bigger things. His secretary had been unusually helpful, and the day progressed smoothly and efficiently.

Later, as Barney is driving home in the same commute traffic, he reflects philosophically, "Well, it's a little crowded, but so what; those people have a right to be on the freeway as much as I do. I'll just listen to some soothing music and unwind a little." Arriving home, Barney sees the same tricycle in the same driveway. Moving it gently out of the way, Barney muses, "Oh well, kids will be kids. I bet the little fellow had a great time playing today."

Guess who's watching TV again as Barney enters the house? Uh-huh, that's right. But listen . . . "Hello, Daddy's home." "That's okay kids, don't get up. Just relax and enjoy yourselves," intones Barney, silently grateful that his kids aren't roaming the streets.

"Honey, I didn't expect you home so soon. I'm afraid dinner's not ready yet," Barney's wife explains apologetically.

The soul of understanding, Barney consoles: "Darling, that's the least of my concerns. You're probably exhausted anyway with the kids and all the housework. Tell you what . . . I'll take the family out to dinner tonight."

Here's an example of two totally different reactions to the same situation by the same individual. The only thing that differed was the amount of stress. Granted that the situation is hypothetical. But can that happen? You bet it can. And it does. What accounts for this "Jekyll and Hyde" performance by Barney? No, Barney's not a multiple personality á la Sybil. He's just exhibiting some of the warning signs of coping burnout.

During those periods of time when your self-esteem is being enhanced, it is much easier to cope. It's simpler to prioritize and keep little things little. Whatever your level of coping ability may be, it is at its best when you are feeling good about yourself and your situation.

The first warning sign that we may be experiencing the start of coping burnout is *Coping Skill Erosion.*

The effect of Coping Skill Erosion is analogous to having a "sunburned psyche." What may be intended as a caress feels like a slap. Little pressures that are normally handled without a thought become overwhelming burdens. As stressors intensify or multiply, coping skills deteriorate further. Increasing irritability and touchiness are common, and the person overreacts to small problems.

Typical coping styles become energized and exaggerated as if in a last-ditch effort to overwhelm the stressor. This leads to distortions in behavior that usually compound the problem and result in vicious cycles. For example, people whose normal behavior is assertive become aggressive and combative. Insult is assumed where none was intended, and they are ready to do battle with minimal provocation.

Those who normally tend toward shyness and withdrawal become more withdrawn. Avoidance mechanisms such as denial increase, further worsening their problems. Excessive drinking, eating, and smoking are likely as the overstressed individual attempts to deal with his short-term anxiety and lack of emotional nourishment.

Included in this erosion of coping ability is the decay of judgment. As stressors continue, the ability to make constructive decisions deteriorates. The pattern of deterioration is also characterized by exaggeration and distortion. People who tend to make quick decisions normally become impulsive and capricious in their judgments. "Sinning in haste," they then "repent at leisure." The more cautious and conservative decision makers develop indecisiveness and self-doubt.

The course and extent of coping erosion is directly related to *1.* the pre-stressed level of coping ability, and *2.* the amount, intensity, and duration of the stressors. Severe stress will erode the coping efficiency of anyone in time. Imagine, then, the effects of stress on those poor unfortunates who, at their best, have marginal coping skills.

I always admire people when they handle a difficult situation well, especially when I can learn something from it. Just the other day, I was in the supermarket when a mother with her young child caught my eye. The child, about four years old, was riding in the "kiddie seat" of the shopping cart while mother did her shopping.

As they roamed the aisles, I couldn't help noticing that the little girl was not overjoyed at being restrained in the cart. She was yelling and screaming, demanding that the mother put her down. I moved closer. "Just be calm, Susan, don't get upset; we'll be leaving in a minute," the mother pleaded. I was truly impressed that this lady was staying calm and attempting to soothe her child but, from the way the kid was behaving, I didn't think she was likely to calm down.

About then, the frustrated child swept her arm down a row of cereal boxes, depositing them on the floor. "Now it's coming," I thought to myself. I listened. "Susan, please be calm. There's no need to get upset. Everyone is watching, so try to be patient," the mother whispered tranquilly. I was really impressed. Most mothers, or anyone else for that matter, would have been at the breaking point by this time. I mean, I was ready to throttle the kid and she wasn't even mine! I felt a glow of admiration for this paragon of composure.

But now it was over. Enough is enough. I knew she had met her Waterloo when one of her child's flailing arms sent a large bottle of pickles crashing to the floor. Have you ever heard a quart of pickles hit the floor?

Shoppers looked on in dismay. The store manager's slow boil was now roiling to the surface. I listened expectantly. I couldn't believe it. Once more her self-possessed supplications filled my ears. "Now, Susan, there's no need to fall apart. Just be calm. Everything will be all right."

Frankly, I was overwhelmed. Approaching the mother, I extolled, "Ma'am, pardon the intrusion, but I couldn't help overhearing the way you were talking to little Susan here. You were splendid. I must commend you on your patience and understanding." She flushed slightly and, with an embarrassed smile, said, "Well thank you, but I don't think you understand. My daughter's name is Katy. *I'm* Susan!"

In all soberness though, it does take a reservoir of strength to retain your poise in the face of increasing stress. Prolonged and intense stress erodes coping strength in an insidious fashion. If stress is not managed successfully, a vicious cycle ensues. As coping skills deteriorate from the prolonged onslaught of the stressor, you become vulnerable to new attacks. Then, as the weakened coping skills invite additional stressors, an accelerating downward spiral develops.

Stress Strategy #4

Develop more coping skills
than you think you will ever need.

THE "BENCH STRENGTH" STRATEGY

Since Coping Skill Erosion is one of the first dangers in dealing with stress, you must have a strategy for it. I call this the "Bench Strength" strategy.

Coaches covet players who, though not on the starting team, can enter a game as needed with minimal, or no, loss in team effectiveness. Teams with such players are said to have depth, or "bench strength." To have bench strength in stress management requires the development of a depth and variety of coping skills.

Every problem becomes easier when you have hundreds of solutions to apply.

Each suicidal patient I've ever treated has told me the same thing: "I don't see any way out." I always respond with the same question: "You mean then that if you had a way to handle the problem you wouldn't want to die?" So far, they have all said, "Of course not!" The lack of alternatives leads to despair. The presence of alternatives gives hope.

Therapy consists of helping them to see, and accept, alternative methods of dealing with their problems. Oh yes, it's a little more involved than that. But the presence of viable alternatives always reduces the severity of stress.

Learning more about yourself and how to live successfully, improving your interpersonal skills, augmenting your vocational skills, acquiring financial management skills, and enhancing your child-raising knowledge, are all examples of life skills that will bolster your coping alternatives. Finally, when something happens to stress you, and you don't have any idea how to cope with it, remember this. There is always an alternative to despair. There is a way. Find it.

The second symptom of Coping Burnout is *Escalating Vulnerability*. This means that when we are under stress, we develop an increasing vulnerability to other stressors. When you are dealing with psychological stress, for example, you are less resistant to *physical* stressors. Have you ever noticed that when you are under a lot of stress, you tend to catch the "bugs" that are going around? As our mind and body attempt to accommodate to, and deal with, psychological stressors, it is as if our body becomes "distracted" by its activity and is vulnerable to attack. You are much more apt to get that latest version of the flu when you are psychologically stressed than when you are relaxed and content.

But we are not just more vulnerable to physical stressors. Being overstressed also makes us more accident-prone. Things just seem to go from bad to worse. Think about it. When you are pressured and frustrated on the job, isn't that when you spill coffee on your suit or dress? That's when you have the "fender bender" backing out of the supermarket parking lot. And you wonder, "Why me, Lord?"

The concept of Escalating Vulnerability is even validated in our folklore. Remember the adages such as "Trouble comes in bunches" and "When it rains it pours." These old sayings testify to an implicit understanding of our increasing vulnerability under stress.

Just as psychological stressors make us more vulnerable to physical stressors, so do physical stressors make us more vulnerable to psychological stressors. I've never met a person yet whose temperament or mood was improved by being ill. Sick people are usually accorded more tolerance and understanding than otherwise allowed. We seem to know that being ill creates a certain kind of emotional fragility and sensitivity.

Some people, of course, may take advantage of this. They make no effort at all, when ill, to curb their irritability and peevishness. They may be grouchy and cantankerous, demanding and petulant, with impunity. And they feel justified in their claim for special attention because "I'm sick!" Of course, you and I don't act that way—just other people.

The escalating vulnerability experienced by physically ill people is more serious than becoming edgy and cranky. Physically ill people are, in fact, more vulnerable to depression and anxiety than physically healthy people. This is a major concern in the treatment of seriously ill patients. Frustrations, pressures, and conflicts normally handled with aplomb may tip the scale against the patient who is using all his resources just to stay alive.

The physically ill person who is happy and loving has a much better chance of getting well, and getting well quicker, than the hateful, vengeful patient.

The biblical admonition to "love your enemies" may owe its origin more to a concern for our own health than the well-being of our enemies. When a patient of mine with bleeding ulcers complained that a certain person "burns me up," I responded with all gravity, "You may be right."

The final payment in the "wages of stress" is *Running out of*

Gas. I have a theory about coping with stress, and it seems to be supported by the research. I call it the "Gas Tank" theory of coping supply.

There is increasing evidence to suggest that we are born with a genetically predetermined amount of stress-coping ability. This limited amount of stress-coping "gas" determines how long we will be able to cope with stress before our body gives out. The amount varies for each individual according to genetic determinates as yet not fully understood. I liken this to being born with a gas tank capable of holding, for example, 100 gallons of stress-coping ability. As I said, the size of the "gas tank" and the number of "gallons" varies with the individual. I'm using the analogy and figure of 100 gallons as an example only.

Every time we cope with a stressor, we use up a little of the "gas." The process of using up the "gas" is called aging. When the "gas" is used up and the tank is empty, the result is death. The more severe the stressors, the less time it takes for the "gas" to be depleted. A stressor is considered severe by its intensity, importance, and duration, and by our level of effectiveness in dealing with it.

In other words, if a stressor is intrinsically severe, it takes more "gas" to deal with it. The Holmes-Rahe Social Readjustment Rating Scale mentioned earlier gives you an idea of the level of severity of various stressors. A stressor also uses more "gas" if we are ineffective in dealing with it. If we agonize over trivial situations and attempt to cope using inadequate methods, then we use more "gas." Even if the stressor is over something substantial, it's important not to waste "gas" by overreacting.

With this in mind, it is of interest to note the change in physical appearance of U.S. Presidents during their term in office. For some of them, the severe stresses of that office have aged them dramatically and graphically. Of course, with a few of them we aren't sure whether it was caused by the level of stress or the level of their incompetency. Probably both.

The average length of time before "running out of gas" can be deduced by looking at actuarial tables. These tables show the average age at the time of "running out of gas," or death. In the United States, it's a little over seventy years, with women living slightly longer than men. Actuarial tables reflect the toll taken by the interaction of physical stressors, such as disease, and psychological stressors.

There is no evidence at this time that you can increase the length of time it takes to "run out of gas." You are born with just so much and when it's gone, it's gone. Jogging, watching your diet, exercise, taking vitamins—nothing can change the length of time that you have. That's the bad news. But before you get too depressed, let me elaborate.

Medical researchers are becoming convinced that our potential longevity is a lot more than is shown by the actuarial tables. In fact, because of the way we "drive our cars," very few, if any, people get the full benefit of their potential longevity. That's where jogging, exercise, etc. enter the picture. More about that later.

It's a little like saying that you may have a high-powered car that uses a lot of gas, or you may have an economy model that gets good mileage. In either case, however, how you drive the car determines whether or not you will get the mileage you are capable of getting.

No matter what size "gas tank" you were born with, one thing is certain. It doesn't make sense to worry so much about running out of gas that you fail to enjoy the trip. In coping with stress, what concerns us primarily is not how much time we have, but how well we use that time.

AREN'T YOU GLAD YOU'RE NOT DUMB . . . LIKE ME?

With those facts in mind, let me make a confession. It's supposed to be good for the soul. At least, it might be helpful to you.

Even though I know that letting myself be stressed needlessly is a waste of my "gas"—even though I know it can cost me moments of my life—I still do it. As a matter of fact, I give moments of my life to people I don't even know!

To understand how I do this wasteful thing, you have to understand something you probably didn't know. I own the freeways in California. I mean I don't mind if someone uses them occasionally, but when I get on them, I expect everyone else to respect my position and . . . MOVE OVER! I'll let them use the slow lane. I simply ask that they get out of my lane.

As I speed along the freeway, eager to get to my destination, sometimes another driver will pull into "my" lane—in front of me—in no hurry to get anywhere. He is preventing me from getting to my destination at the appointed time. This is an unconscionable violation and must not be tolerated. But I'm not completely unreasonable. I realize that he may not have heard of my ownership position. So I tell him.

Now it's hard to talk on the freeway, so I have a technique of communication that I use to get his attention. I press the accelerator and speed toward his bumper. At the last minute, I hit the brakes and the horn. He notices. Then I motion to him, informing him of my ownership, and politely encourage him to get out of my lane. You'd be surprised to learn how many people don't appreciate that courtesy. He slows down.

Talk about frustration!

Now it's serious. He's defied my authority and must be informed of his transgression. We can't talk, so I use sign language. I signify the number of his legitimate parents—or the level of his IQ. I don't care; he can take it anyway he wants to.

Responding to my attempts to communicate, he signals back. Within seconds, my hands are gripping the steering wheel with white knuckles, the veins are distended on my neck, and I am leaning over the wheel, mouthing obscenities. Stressed? You bet I am. I'm on the way to an accident. Possibly a cerebrovascular accident.

How can this incident do so much to me? I'm frustrated, upset, ready for a fight. I'm not fit company for saner people, and you can imagine what I'll be like when I get where I'm going. By telling myself that his failure to recognize my ownership of the freeways is an insult, or that I will suffer a calamitous delay, I turn a harmless trivium into a life-threatening event.

Does calling it life-threatening sound like an overreaction? Consider this. Permitting myself to be stressed by *any* event uses up my "gas" in an amount proportionate to the stress. And remember, I have a limited quantity of stress-coping energy in my "gas tank." When it's gone, it's gone. No refills. It's similar to revving your engine with the car in neutral. You're not going anywhere, it impresses no one, and it's a waste of gas.

I am therefore spending moments of my life on a situation providing no benefit to anyone. Especially me. By catastrophizing trivialities over a period of years, I can appreciably shorten my life! That makes it life-threatening. And for whom? Someone I don't even know!

Aren't you glad you're not dumb like that?

It's worse than that. Not only have I spent precious moments of my life being stressed by people I don't even know but I have done it for people I don't even like!

For instance, a friend of mine may report to me that a person I don't like has been saying negative things about me. Now you would think that, since I don't even like this person, the last thing I would want to do is give him some of my allotted time. Wrong! I fuss and fume for a couple of days over the injustice of his actions. I tell anyone who will listen what a horrible human being my enemy is. In short, I'm perfectly miserable for a couple of days permitting myself to be stressed over someone *I don't even like!*

Getting emotionally distraught and revengeful over what someone says about you can shorten your life. It causes you to use your irreplaceable stress-coping energy supply which depletes your "gas tank." Remember, when it's gone, it's gone. There are no refills. The stations are closed. It's just not worth it.

Aren't you glad you're not dumb like me?

As we study the effects of stress, the injunction to "love your enemies" makes more and more sense. Far from being simply a virtuous, do-gooder philosophy of life, it looks increasingly like altruistic self-regard. In fact, Dr. Hans Selye calls this strategy, "altruistic egoism." However, there is a more cynical paraphrase of "love your enemies" that tickles my funnybone: "Love your enemies; it drives them crazy."

Whatever your motivation to not waste your "gas," it's the results that count. If you, as a reasonably mature person, were asked to give up a year of your life for someone you didn't know or like, you would undoubtedly refuse. No one would blame you. Does it make sense, then, to waste your stress-coping energy over people who aren't important to you? Of course not.

Naturally, all people are important. But not all situations are important. It's necessary to discriminate between the trivial and the significant and put your energy where it counts. If you don't, you'll end up imitating the last, and worst, part of my confession.

Not only do I waste my "gas" on people I don't even know and people I don't even like, I have nothing left for people I love.

All day long, I work hard to handle problems. Some of them with people I don't know and people I don't like. All day long, I become stressed with things I can't control anyway, and with business problems that will always be there. Then I go home. There are the people I know, like, and love; and there's nothing left. These are the ones who catch the fallout from my burnout. I'm irritable, oversensitive, and grouchy—and with the ones who are the most important people in the world to me.

Now, aren't you glad you're not dumb like that?

If you value your family, then you want to devote as much of your stress-coping energy to them as you can. If you use all your gas driving strangers and enemies around town, you won't have any left to take your family anywhere.

Every time you cope with a stressor, you use up irreplaceable energy. Frequently I hear people say, "Yes, but I can't help it. Some things just make me upset." Some people apparently feel they have no choice in deciding what is going to upset them. If you believe that, try this. To every potentially stressful situation, ask yourself this question, "Do I really want to empty my gas tank for this?" If you do this, you will soon marvel at how many times you really do have a choice.

That stress-coping energy you have is limited and precious. Doesn't it make sense to spend it wisely? Follow the fifth strategy for stress.

Stress Strategy #5

Save your stress-coping energy
for things that really count.

This means getting your priorities straight — then learning to ignore the trivial and focus on the significant. The priority of values you select is, of course, entirely up to you. But whatever your values are, if you concentrate your stress-coping energy on them, you will feel a greater sense of satisfaction with your life. I'm not suggesting that this is easy to do. It's not. It's difficult. So difficult that, with many people, the reverse is frequently true. They ignore the significant and focus on the trivial.

This becomes true with people who have never thought seriously about what they really believe in. They haven't clarified their values. Maybe this is so because it seems too hard, or perhaps they simply don't know how.

I've found two methods that work. They have a high potential for straightening out priorities: getting old, and becoming terminally ill.

I once had a patient who went through life like a steamroller. He ran roughshod over anyone or anything that stood in his way. His number one goal was "making a buck." He didn't care what he did, or who he did it to, as long as he had more dollars afterward than before. His family was suffering from his emotional neglect and abuse. He either didn't notice or didn't care.

I tried everything to reach him. Nothing worked.

One day, he came into my office with a much softer look on his face. He expressed regret over his past behavior and vowed he would be different. He cried as he told me how distant he felt from his family. He hardly knew his kids, and he and his wife were like two strangers living together. He lamented the wasted years and determined that he would concentrate on pulling his family back together again. He now realized what was really important to him, he said, and he wanted to correct the damage to his relationships if he possibly could. What a change!

"What happened to make this change in you?" I asked. He then told me that three days earlier, his physician had told him he had discovered a fast-growing cancer. He had given him six months to live. With only a few months to live, he had discovered that his relationship with his family was more important than he realized.

Yes, terminal illness is a marvelous way to clarify your values.

Another good method is to get old. As people face the final years of their lives, they commonly find that their values become restructured. They learn to discriminate between the trivial and the significant. They then see clearly how they should have spent their lives and where they should have put their energy. Getting old is another effective method of clarifying your values.

It's amazing how facing your own death can put your priorities in order and supply the motivation to keep them there.

You may have already noticed, however, one tiny drawback to these two value-clarification methods. By the time they work, you don't have much time left to do anything about it.

There are better ways to prioritize your values. Start by asking yourself some questions. What would you miss the most if you lost it? Who would you miss the most if you lost them? What are the issues that will make a difference in your long-term contentment and happiness? What do you believe in, and what is most important to you? When you get the answers, write them down.

Now analyze a week of activities. List the activities and count the hours you devote to each one. No one's watching, so give yourself an honest answer. Compare your list of values to the list of activities and the time spent on them. Do they match? Are you spending the most time on what you say you value the most?

A story is told of Alexander the Great and an event that occurred during one of his battles. A soldier accused of cowardice in the face of the enemy was brought to him for judgment. The soldier was just a lad of about fifteen. The boy stood in front of the great general, trembling in fear. "What is your name?" asked the legendary conqueror. "My name," the soldier said hesitantly, "is Alexander." Alexander the Great spoke softly with suppressed rage: "Son, you either change your name, or change your ways."

If what you say you value doesn't jibe with how you spend your time, the decision is this: Either change your values or change your behavior.

I have values that I profess to live by. But, like you, I don't always do it. I need help keeping life in perspective. One of the aids I use to help keep my priorities in alignment is the axiom, "People are more important than things, and things are important only insofar as they help people."

I would love to come to the end of my life knowing that whatever amount of "gas" I entered this world with, I spent it on values that counted. I don't want to lose a drop to regret. I know, that's idealistic. But it keeps my focus clear and my purpose center stage. I am convinced that the attempt, by itself, will enrich my life and the lives of my loved ones.

Chapter Seven

Building Your Stress Survival Quotient (SSQ)

The "Gas Tank" theory says that nothing you can do will change the size of your gas tank. Neither jogging, diet, nor any other health practice will give you any more "gas." You're born with just so much "gas," and when you run out, you die.

Becoming aware of the "Gas Tank" theory causes some people to adopt a fatalistic attitude. Their feeling is, "If I have a genetically predetermined amount of stress-coping energy, then it doesn't make much difference what I do." "Why should I get all sweaty if exercise doesn't help? Why should I starve myself or do anything that's supposed to be good for me—but no fun—if it's a waste of time?" Logical questions, indeed. Believing this, they can justify any type of excess on the grounds that it won't change anything anyway.

That's a mistake, because jogging, diet, and other health practices do make a difference. Sound like a contradiction? Not really. Those health-building attempts do have a positive effect, but not by increasing your stress-coping energy quota. They help by increasing your body's resistance to stress.

While it is impossible to escape all of the ravages of stress, you are definitely able to increase your resistance to its aftermath.

This is different than the resistance mentioned in The Stress Formula. Remember that? Force plus Resistance equals Stress. The resistance described in The Stress Formula referred to the level of flexibility we have in our coping styles. Increasing your resistance to stress is something I prefer to think of as your Stress Survival Quotient. This concerns your ability to use all the "gas" you have potentially available. You can think of it as living longer and better, or, getting an engine tune-up.

TUNING YOUR ENGINE

The fact is that your potential for meaningful longevity may be greater than your present life expectancy. Most people never get to use the full potential of their "gas tank" because of poor health habits. Put more simply, you may have the potential to live 100 years, but only get to age 50 because of the way you live.

Imagine that you decided to go on an important trip in your car. Since there are no gas stations along the way, getting good mileage is essential to you. After all, you don't want to run out of gas before the trip is over. Knowing that there were no service stations along the way would make you more concerned about the condition of your car than you might ordinarily be. Would you want to drive a car badly in need of a tune-up? Of course not. The car wouldn't burn the gas efficiently and you wouldn't reach your destination.

Traveling through life is a lot like that hypothetical automobile trip. The destination is the full use of your life potential. You only have one car (body), there are no gas stations, and the kind of condition you keep your body in will determine whether you complete the trip.

That's where exercise, proper diet, and other health practices come into the picture. They don't give you more "gas," but they do help "tune up" your engine so that you get to use all you have, and use it efficiently.

The effective management of stress involves more than just dealing with its consequences through relaxation and other techniques. A primary goal of any comprehensive stress-management program must emphasize increasing your Stress Survival Quotient—your resistance to stress. That means learning how to tune up your engine so you can get every year that's coming to you.

Of course, there's more to life than the length of it. But why not live longer if you're living fully? I'm in favor of quality in preference to quantity but, when it comes to life, I'll take both.

MEDDLIN' WITH YOUR HEALTH

My father was a minister. A good portion of his ministerial career was as an evangelist. Some of you know exactly what I'm talking about when I say I cut my teeth on a pew and grew up with sawdust in my pockets and cuffs. Revival meetings.

Now there are basically two kinds of evangelists: those who get you all excited about going to heaven, and those who make you scared to death that you're going to hell. The latter type are known as the "hellfire and brimstone" preachers.

We had a little old lady, Aunt Agnes, who attended our church. Aunt Agnes just loved revival meetings. She especially loved the "hellfire and brimstone" preachers. "Tell it like it is. . . ," she would shout, ". . . call sin, sin."

We had a hellfire evangelist come to our church once who was really good. He could make hell so hot that, as he preached, your pew felt warmer. You were sure that you could smell the sulphur in the air. People were lining up to get "saved" so they wouldn't have to go to that awful place. Some did it more than once, just to be sure.

Aunt Agnes couldn't get enough. Didn't miss a night.

One evening, the evangelist was really on a roll. ". . . And all those people who drink that rotgut whiskey are going to hell," he admonished. Aunt Agnes was responding in concert with him. "Preach it, brother," she encouraged as she nudged her neighbor.

". . . And all those people who smoke them cancer sticks is going to hell," he warned. "Preach it, brother," said Aunt Agnes, giving her neighbor another nudge. ". . . And all those people who go to them filthy movie shows is going to hell," he continued with increasing passion. Right in rhythm with voice and elbow, Aunt Agnes shouted again, "Preach it, brother." ". . . And all them people that dips that snuff is going to hell."

Aunt Agnes was coldly quiet.

Then, leaning toward her neighbor, she grumbled, "Now he's quit preachin' and gone to meddlin'."

Aunt Agnes is like a lot of people. They can easily see the virtue of other people changing their destructive health habits, but they are blind to their own. If you want to fine-tune your engine for maximum mileage, you will probably have to make some adjustments. That means "meddlin' " with your health habits.

1. NUTRITION

No thinking person will dispute that there is a direct relationship between diet and health. To be sure, there are differences of opinion on specific issues such as the value of vitamin supplements, certain types of foods, and the type of diet that is best. But on one issue there is general consensus. All things being equal, a healthy diet promotes a healthy body. Proper nutrition increases your Stress Survival Quotient because a healthy body is more resistant to the effects of stress.

What is a healthy diet? Who knows? I'm not a nutritionist, so I don't know. Nutritionists frequently disagree with one another, so I wonder if they even know. About the time we think we have the answers, a new study brings up more questions, and I wonder if anybody really knows.

That turns a lot of people away from actively pursuing a healthy diet. There's just too much confusing, and sometimes conflicting, information to assimilate.

But, wait a minute. It's true we don't have all the answers yet, but some consistent facts have begun to emerge. Abiding by a few of these proven diet recommendations seems to make sense if you're serious about increasing your SSQ. There is one time-honored cliché that I recommend, with just a few elaborations. Eat a balanced diet. The key here is moderation. Avoiding excesses in either the amount or the type of food ingested is proven nutritional wisdom. Some of the excesses to be avoided are agreed on by any competent authority in nutrition.

A. Fatty Foods   There is little doubt in anyone's mind of the dangers of a fatty diet. The potential for arteriosclerosis, the so-called hardening of the arteries leading to increased cardiac risk, is proven. Your heart has enough strain on it dealing with stress without having to work under a handicap.

The American Heart Association has sponsored numerous studies showing a definite relationship between a fatty diet and cardiac problems. A fatty diet and the chances of your ending up on the operating table or suffering a heart attack, stroke, or other cardiovascular problem, are clearly correlated. These diseases afflict more than 63 million Americans, and kill more of us than any other single cause of death.

Cholesterol is one form of dietary fat. It is found in the blood in fat-protein combinations known as lipoproteins. In 1984, The National Institute of Health published the results of a ten-year study on heart disease and a fatty diet. This study plainly demonstrated a reduction in heart attacks and heart disease in people who reduced their cholesterol levels. In spite of this dramatic evidence, more than 50% of middle-aged (45-65) Americans have cholesterol levels in the danger zone associated with heart disease.

The typical American has a serum cholesterol level of about 230. Men with this level will suffer their first (and possibly last) heart attack by age 70. Women with this level will suffer their first by age 75. Your physician may call your serum cholesterol level normal anywhere up to 300. But at a serum cholesterol level of 300, the first heart attack may be expected at age 54 for men and 58 for women.

Remember, the words typical and normal only mean average. They don't necessarily mean healthy. In Japan, where heart disease rates are much lower than in America, the "normal" or average cholesterol level is below 200. If your serum cholesterol level was at that figure, it would extend your estimated heart attack age to 81 for men and 86 for women.

Keep in mind that cholesterol is just one form of dietary fat. It seems to get all the bad press, but all other types of fat are also dangerous to your health, taken in excess. Excess is a word that exemplifies the diet of many Americans. It has been determined that forty percent of the average American's caloric intake is obtained from fat. That is excess with a capital E!

I realize that it's highly unlikely that you will go to the extreme of some of the popular no-fat and low-fat diets, no matter how healthful they may be. But at least move in the direction of moderation. Most people seem willing to play Russian roulette with their diets and resist all the warnings about a fatty diet. That's fine as long as you don't kid yourself about the chances you are taking. It's your life and it's your business. However, you could probably reduce your intake of red meats, butter, and other sources of fats without losing the pleasure you get from eating one bit. Try it. You might like it; and the health benefits are a real plus.

B. Sugar and Spice, and Everything Nice Don't you just hate it when everything you like the most turns out to be bad for you? Things like sugar and caffeine come in delicious and appealing forms. For some people, the need for them borders on an addiction. For a few, there's no border about it. They have to have it! So go ahead and do it. You probably will anyway. Just don't kid yourself.

The next time you have a bad morning, ask yourself this question: "Is there any relationship between my cranky, irritable, somewhat depressed feelings, and the three cups of coffee and sweet roll I had for breakfast?"

Be aware of the danger of carbohydrate jags. The excessive intake of simple carbohydrates, like sugar, can lead to volatility in emotion and energy. The pattern starts with an acceleration of heart and pulse rate combined with agitation and a lowered tolerance for frustration. That means you feel restless, cranky, and irritable.

Then your body starts to assimilate the sugars and begins to move downward. Unfortunately, it doesn't stop in the middle. It continues on down to a temporary hypoglycemia (low blood sugar) with the consequent lessening of energy, and vulnerability to depression.

Not to worry. Just pop a couple of Twinkies and you can start the process all over again. Combine all this with caffeine and it's like throwing pine needles on a bonfire. With very little effort, you can develop some vicious mood swings and a destructive cycle that can set a pernicious pattern for your personality as well as your health.

Since the average American consumes 126 pounds of sugar a year, the potential for this type of problem is great. The typical American child's breakfast is so heavy with sugar that learning and behavior problems can be predicted in the absence of any other indicators such as family, intelligence, or perceptual-motor problems.

When you're dealing with stress, you already have tendencies toward irritability and depression. You certainly don't want to compound the problem with excessive sugar and caffeine. Combining stress, sugars, and caffeine is a black-edged invitation to personal health disaster. Besides, simple sugars and caffeine increase triglycerides, another form of blood fat, and fatty acids. You already know what a fatty diet does. Who needs it?

C. Leave the Salt in the Ocean   With hypertension (i.e., high blood pressure) at almost-epidemic proportions, you need to take a serious look at your intake of salt. Excess sodium is clearly an adverse factor in some, if not most, people prone to hypertension. It is also implicated in excess gastric acid secretion, stomach cancer, atherosclerosis, cerebrovascular disease, and migraine headaches.

According to the National Academy of Sciences publication, *Recommended Dietary Allowances*, average salt consumption in the U.S. is estimated at from 6 to 18 grams a day. However, the average human requirement is about ½ gram a day. Chances are your regular diet gives you that much in the canned and packaged foods you eat, without adding table salt. The Senate Select Committee on Nutrition and Human Needs recommends that your intake of salt not exceed 3 grams a day. The goal of 3 grams of salt a day amounts to about ³/₅ of a teaspoon.

Think about this. There are 2000 milligrams of sodium in one teaspoon of salt. (Salt is about 40% sodium.) The recommended maximum for sodium is 1200 milligrams. One tablespoon of catsup plus salt on just 10 french fries would result in sodium ingestion of about 370 milligrams or about 25% of the recommended maximum. The same french fries without salt would only contain 2 milligrams of sodium. Since it is probable that your regular diet already supplies your daily requirement, the salt from the shaker is working against your health. Whether you are under stress or not, your blood pressure doesn't need any more help in going up.

As I said before, I doubt that you will go on a salt-free diet. Okay. No problem. It's your life and it's your business. Just don't kid yourself. Your use of table salt may be a danger—and an unnecessary danger—to your health. Aside from elevating your blood pressure and increasing other health risks, it doesn't do your kidneys any good either.

Would you like to cut down? Try a couple of tricks that I find helpful. Do you ever find yourself reaching for the saltshaker before you have even tasted your food? Uh-huh. Me too. Try this instead. Get in the habit of simply tasting your food before you reach for the salt. Then only add it if it really needs it. Ask yourself the question, "Does it really need salt or is this just a habit?"

Better yet, don't put salt on the table. Make yourself get up and get it if something just has to have some salt. It will help your decision process. Another technique that I use a lot is to use lemon juice in my cooking instead of salt. It adds the zip that you get from salt without the disadvantages.

I've read that the typical American eats an average of 5.3 times a day. (I've concluded they only counted adult Americans, because my two teenage boys eat more times than that before breakfast!) Anyway, that works out to slightly more than 1,934 times a year. How many of those 1900-plus times are you putting garbage in your body? See what I mean? Your diet may very well be the single biggest influence on your health and your ability to cope with stress. At the very least, it's worth "meddlin'" with and making a few changes.

You don't have to be an expert in nutrition to figure out that people are a lot like computers in one regard—GIGO. Garbage In, Garbage Out. You can't feed your body junk and expect it to handle stress in an optimum fashion.

The U.S. government (doing something right for a change) published some sensible and simple guidelines a few years ago. In 1977, the Senate Select Committee released their study entitled *Dietary Goals for the United States.* They recommended a diet with reductions in cholesterol, refined and processed sugars, salt, alcohol (ouch!), and calories; and increases in complex carbohydrates and roughage.

Is it worth the trouble?

Nutritional experts have estimated that if everyone would follow this diet, there would be an 80% reduction in obesity, 25% less heart disease, a 50% drop or improvement in cases of diabetes, and an annual increase in longevity of 1%. That means after ten years of this diet, you would live ten percent longer!

Not convinced yet? The *Journal of the National Cancer Institute* contained something that should interest you. This study suggested that 35% of all cancer deaths might be avoided by changes in diet! Included in that were 90% fewer deaths from stomach and large-bowel cancers, and 50% fewer deaths from breast and uterine cancer.

Worth it? You bet it is!

Increasing the health of your body by modifying your diet along these practical guidelines is a highly effective strategy for stress.

This isn't a book about nutrition and you may wish to explore the role of nutrition further. There are several sensible, readable, research-based books on nutrition at your bookstore. One I recommend is *The Target Diet* by Covert Bailey. Even if you don't follow it exactly, it provides a good model to keep you moving in the right direction.

2. WEIGHT AND YOUR SSQ

Another method of increasing your SSQ, and closely related to nutrition, is to keep your weight within healthy limits. The health risk involved in being overweight has been heralded so much in the last ten years that you would have to be from another planet not to be aware of it. But aside from the esthetic and physical advantages of being at the proper weight, there are even more important concerns: your ability to survive stress. The major issue in being overweight, as it relates to surviving stress, is increased vulnerability to heart attacks.

When your body began to develop in the womb after conception, it grew according to an exact genetic blueprint. Your heart was designed to support the skeletal size and proportionate body weight predetermined by this blueprint. All other factors being equal, you should achieve and maintain that ideal weight for maximum cardiac efficiency and longevity.

Any weight over your ideal weight is more than your blueprint called for, and your body has to make changes to accommodate the extra weight. It's like inviting an extra guest to dinner—you have to have enough to go around. So, for every ten pounds you are overweight, your body creates about 15,000 additional blood vessels to feed the fat. Your heart has to pump blood through those "extra" vessels and that means it has to work harder. Your genetic blueprint provided for your heart to handle a certain weight for a certain length of time. If it has to work harder by handling more than it was built to handle, it may not be able to work as long. For example, if your car gets 20 miles to the gallon at 4000 pounds, it follows that it will get less mileage at a higher weight. So will you.

If you maintain a weight that is 20% over your ideal weight, you have an 80% chance of having a major health breakdown by age 50. If you are 30% overweight, you have a 100% chance of a major health breakdown by age 50. If you are significantly overweight, don't just listen to the ticking of the time bomb, do something! The issue is not to increase your worthiness; you are already priceless. It is not to make you more attractive; you look great. The issue is your survival.

The classic Framingham study has examined a group of patients for more than thirty years. Their report shows that, independent of other risk factors, the degree of obesity is clearly correlated with increased risk of coronary artery disease and a shorter life span.

Maintaining your ideal weight is a critical factor in your ability to survive stress. That will free your body of many burdens and liberate energy to cope with stress.

But what is your ideal weight?

There are all kinds of charts and tables you could consult, but for accuracy and simplicity, here's the method I prefer:

> *MEN:* For the first five feet of height, you should weigh 100 pounds. For every inch over

five feet (60 inches), add six pounds to compute your ideal weight. For example, the average height of the American male is five feet nine and three-fourths inches. Let's round it off to 5′ 10″. That works out to 70 inches. Add 100 pounds for the first 60 inches and 6 pounds per inch for the next 10 inches. That creates an ideal weight for a 5′ 10″ American male of 160 pounds.

WOMEN: For women, the figures are similar with one difference. It is 100 pounds for the first 60 inches, but for every inch over that, add only 5 pounds. Since the average height of the American woman is 5′ 5″, that computes to an ideal weight of 125 pounds.

Now, just plug in those figures to your height and you will come up with the ideal weight for your height.

"But, wait a minute," you say. "What if you have big bones?" (Ever notice that most fat people have big bones?) But it's true, there are differences in skeleton size and that has an effect. So allow a 10% variation for skeletal size.

Applied to our example of the average American male, what does that mean? Well, his ideal weight is 160 pounds. Ten percent of 160 is sixteen. That means the maximum healthy weight for a large-framed 5′ 10″ American male is 176 pounds. The 5′ 5″ woman should weigh 125 pounds. Ten per cent of that is 12½ pounds. The maximum weight for a 5′ 5″ large-framed woman is 137½ pounds.

The longitudinal Framingham study, from which we derive much of our knowledge about obesity and the heart, revealed that being underweight could also increase cardiac risk. Therefore, using the figures in our example, the minimum that a 5' 10" small-framed American man should weigh is 144 pounds. The minimum weight for a small-framed 5' 5" woman is 112½ pounds.

The key element in deriving salutary benefits from maintaining your proper weight is the word "maintaining." All the evidence suggests that large weight loss fluctuations may be just as damaging to your health as chronic obesity. You don't do your body any good by gaining and losing weight with each new "fad" diet that comes along. Get it off and keep it off.

3. EXERCISE

It has been known for years that passive, sedentary types suffer from the effects of stress more than their active counterparts. This leads to the logical conclusion that exercise can increase your SSQ.

Exercise, as a means of preparing the body for athletic endeavor, is standard operating procedure. It is accepted sports wisdom that the better the physical conditioning, the better the athletic performance. If exercise prepares the body to handle the rigors of athletic performance, why wouldn't it prepare the body to handle the rigors of stress? Well, it does.

Health enthusiasts have long believed that regular, moderate exercise can not only prolong life, but enhance its quality as well.

Now there is proof.

A study, published in March 1986 by the *New England Journal of Medicine,* clearly demonstrates what exercise buffs hold sacred. States the principal author, Dr. Ralph Paffenbarger of the Stanford University School of Medicine, "For each hour of physical activity, you can expect to live that hour over—and live one or two more hours to boot."

Notice the earlier pairing of the word exercise with regular and moderate? That is a key element in deriving maximum benefit from exercise. The researchers found that regular, moderate exercise was a critical factor in determining longevity.

The amount of energy expended, i.e., calories burned off, was positively correlated with increased longevity up to a point. One mile of vigorous walking burns off 100 calories. Men who walked about nine miles a week (900 calories) had a 21% lower risk of death than those who walked three miles or less. The maximum benefit occurred at about 3500 calories a week. This is the equivalent of walking 35 miles a week, or six to eight hours of strenuous bicycling or singles tennis. The subjects who worked out that much had 50% less risk of death compared to those who engaged in little or no exercise.

A surprising revelation was that after 3500 calories of energy were expended, there were diminishing returns. Men who exercised more than that on a weekly basis had higher death rates than their more moderate colleagues. The risk of death was also high for ex-varsity athletes who either continued high levels of activity or dropped off dramatically. Quoting the report: "Evidently, inheritance of a sturdy constitution (as implied by varsity athletic status) is less important to longevity than continuation of adequate lifetime exercise."

Another revelation of the study was that a lifetime habit of engaging in energetic activity three to four times a week could actually reduce the negative health effects of cigarette smoking or high blood pressure. It even partly offset an inherited tendency toward early death.

Isn't it remarkable how often regularity and moderation play such central roles in effective living?

While the study is exciting, it should be interpreted with restraint. It is limited in its general application because the research subjects did not reflect a diverse cross-sampling. The study group included only white, male Harvard graduates. Nonetheless, it provides considerable impetus to a growing body of evidence showing the long-term benefits of exercise.

The *Journal of the American Medical Association* published a study that scored points for exercise as a "quality of life" enhancer. This study, directed by Dr. Nancy Lane of Stanford, revealed no difference in joint disease between long-distance runners and non-runners. That's good news for runners and potential runners who are concerned about possible joint damage from running.

Furthermore, their runners, aged 50 to 72, had 40% higher bone density than the sedentary group. That supports other research showing that stressing the skeletal structure tends to strengthen bone tissue. And that's especially good news for women who tend to develop osteoporosis after menopause.

A similar study at the University of Florida, Gainsville, added more support. Dr. Panush, in summarizing the findings, concluded, " . . . Putting a normal joint through the normal range of motion is not harmful. . . . Running may include pounding and wear and tear, but it does not necessarily cause arthritis."

Yes, regular, moderate exercise can substantially increase your SSQ.

MORE MEDDLIN'

1. Smoking   You smokers knew we'd get around to this sooner or later, didn't you? First, the good news. Nicotine, in very small amounts, acts as a mild stimulant but, in larger amounts, it begins to exert a tranquilizing effect which can reduce tension. Also, smokers follow procedures in their smoking behavior that border on ritualistic. These patterned sequences of behavior are characteristic of compulsions and, like compulsive behavior, tend to bind anxiety. Small wonder, then, that during times of stress, smokers tend to smoke more.

Now, the bad news.

If I offered you a delicious gourmet dinner for ten million dollars, you would make a predictable response: "That's too much to pay. I can get the same meal for 100 dollars." The same thing is true with smoking. You do get some tension-reduction benefits, but it costs too much.

It has been estimated that, all other factors being equal, *each cigarette you smoke costs eight minutes of your life.* This estimate reflects the potential danger from cancer, respiratory and heart disease. For a two-pack-a-day smoker, that amounts to a shortened life expectancy of over 40 days a year. That means that for every ten years you smoke two packs a day, you lose one year of your life. Isn't that a little too high a price for a small amount of tension-reduction, especially when there are dozens of other cost-free methods to reduce tension?

In terms of potential damage to your heart, the cost can be even higher. Researcher Forrest Blanding, in his book *Pulse Point Plan,* analyzes health habits to produce estimates of an individual's "coronary age." The term coronary age is used to refer to the age when we *first* can be diagnosed as suffering from coronary disease and such symptoms as angina, abnormal heartbeat, or even heart attack. The coronary age for the average American man is 73; for the average woman, it is 78. According to Blanding's estimates, based on research from more than 200 studies, smoking 20 cigarettes a day lowers your coronary age by two years; 30 a day, by four years; and 50 a day, by six years. That's expensive.

Since I am aware that to many people the word "grass" means more than just something you mow, we need to discuss another kind of smoking—marijuana. This drug is so commonly used by people who otherwise exercise reasonable restraint in their health habits that it has to be discussed.

These smokers justify their marijuana use by saying, among other things, that marijuana relaxes them. They claim that it is good for them because they are under a lot of stress and they need the relaxation it provides. Once again, I ask the question, "But at what cost?" Each marijuana "joint" is, on the average, ten times more carcinogenic than a cigarette. That danger is exclusive of the other neurological and psychological risks, and there are plenty. Can you really afford that?

2. Alcohol   Now we have arrived at the part where I want to say, "Now he's quit preachin' and gone to meddlin'." I am an inveterate oenophile. That, of course, is just a fancy word for a wine snob—and I guess I am. I love tasting the wines I collect for my cellar just as much as I enjoy collecting them. But, like you, I am not immune to the consequences of my behavior. Although, in terms of your SSQ, the consequences may be a little different from what you expected.

There is both expected news and surprising news about alcohol consumption. The expected news is that people who consume moderate amounts of alcohol live longer than those who are immoderate in their consumption. The surprising news is that they also live longer than abstainers. The moderate consumption of alcohol is more salubrious than drinking too much, but it also appears to have a more beneficial effect than not drinking at all. The key word again, as with so many things, is moderate.

Unfortunately, you don't get to define moderate for yourself. One person's moderate could be another person's delirium tremens. Here's what the research suggests as a "rule of thumb" for gauging the amount of alcohol that is regarded as moderate. Moderate daily consumption is considered to be two one-ounce highballs, two six-ounce glasses of table wine, or two twelve-ounce bottles or cans of beer.

Before some of the more creative drinkers get carried away, let me caution you. Your choices are either-or, not all of the above.

One further caveat. You can't save up for a rainy day. One fellow approached me after a lecture on this topic. He was beaming from ear to ear. "Doc'," he said, "am I ever going to have myself a time. I'm not going to drink for a whole month, then I'm going to take all those drinks I've saved up and have a weekend that you wouldn't believe!" Well, you can imagine his chagrin when I clarified for him that the amounts were not cumulative.

Alcohol has the effect of depressing the central nervous system. Since in moderate amounts that simply relaxes the body, it is probable that the increased longevity is a function of regular daily relaxation. I don't mean the type of relaxation that comes from laying around or sitting in an easy chair. Those activities may be relaxing and they have their place, but for real physiological benefit, another type of relaxation is necessary. This form of relaxation has been termed "the relaxation response" and is discussed in Chapter Ten. The point here, however, is that imbibing moderate amounts of alcohol creates a physiological response similar to it.

3. Sleep Deprivation of sleep increases one's vulnerability to stress. Prisoners of war have been "broken" by nothing more complex than sleep deprivation. Volunteers who were deprived of sleep for 72 to 98 hours showed increasing disorganization of behavior as the sleep loss progressed. They were also confused about what time it was and where they were.

Sleep studies have shown that normal adults go through four stages of sleep, extending from light sleep to progressively deeper sleep. They spend about 20 percent of this sleep in Stage 1, considered the main stage for dreaming, and in which rapid eye movement (REM) occurs. About 60 percent is spent in the intermediary Stages 2 and 3, and about 20 percent in the deep sleep of Stage 4. Although some types of dreams may be experienced in Stages 2, 3, and 4, they are referred to as non-rem (NREM) sleep. The typical pattern is for the individual to go through all four stages in about 90 minutes, from light sleep to deep sleep and back again to light sleep.

William Dement, in his sleep research at Stanford, found that deprivation of REM sleep could trigger a mental breakdown in a psychologically vulnerable person. Curiously, most sleeping pills do precisely that; they prevent REM sleep. This results in the phenomenon of sleeping pill users who report that they sleep, but they don't feel rested.

Many physically and mentally ill patients show disturbances in sleep patterns, and it is probable that disturbed sleep patterns play an interactive role in both the problem and its cause.

The moral is apparent. Sleep is a necessary restorative to both mind and body and is an important method of increasing your SSQ. Good, healthy sleep habits help the mind and the body resist the ravages of excessive stress.

Stress Strategy #6

*Take good care of your body
and your health habits so that you have
a head start against stress.*

THE SSQ AND YOUR MENTAL HEALTH

Closing and locking the front door to keep out the burglar isn't very effective if you leave the back door open. The best physical health in the world does little for you if you are not strong mentally. Much of this book pertains to critical issues in mental health, but I want to briefly emphasize two additional areas that you need to be aware of, and protect.

1. Self-Esteem Self-esteem refers to the value that you place on yourself; the sense of worth that you have as a person.

109

It is one of the few things that exemplify the axiom, "You can't have too much of a good thing." It has nothing to do with egotism. The egotist has little regard for others, but he has no love for himself either. The egotist's exaggerated sense of self-worth is merely camouflage for a poorly constructed self-image. The individual with true self-love is fully capable of valuing and loving others equally. The self-loving person's creed might be, "I am a person of worth and value and so are you."

Self-esteem is to the personality what good health is to the body. It is the condition under which maximum growth, development, and participation with life can take place. Self-esteem and vulnerability to stress are inversely correlated. When your self-esteem is low, your vulnerability to stress is high. When your self-esteem is high, your vulnerability to stress is low.

Frequently, stress and self-esteem interact volatilely. Temporary reductions of self-esteem, such as not getting a raise or promotion, increase vulnerability to stress. Negative responses to stress, such as excessive anger, further undermine self-esteem, and a downward spiral ensues. Building and maintaining adequate levels of self-esteem is an invaluable means of increasing your SSQ.

2. Having a Sense of Meaning and Purpose to Your Life
It has been said that the three great questions in life that must be answered in order for there to be any real happiness are, Who Am I?, Where Am I Going?, and Why?

Viktor Frankl, in recounting his experiences in the concentration camps of World War II, declared that the inmates with the highest survival rates were those with the strongest sense of values and purpose. In short, he observed that those who knew who they were, and who had a real reason to live, survived.

A sense of meaning and purpose to life produces hope, and hope is the antidote to depression. Reports from prisoner of war camps tell of cases where prisoners without a sense of meaning and purpose would simply pull the blankets over their heads and wait to die. The prisoners who had a sense of significance and purpose to their lives, transcending mere physical survival, were the ones who were able to endure the torture and deprivation of their imprisonment. Inspirational books abound with stories of medical patients who survived severe illnesses and injuries against the odds. They lived because they wanted to live. They had a sense of meaning and purpose to their lives.

Before the days of mechanized farming, the old-time farmers used homespun wisdom to assist them in accomplishing their goals. One of their techniques was to tie a bandanna to a fence post at the end of the field. They would then move to the opposite end and prepare to plow a furrow. As they guided the mule pulling the plow, they kept their eye firmly fixed on the distant bandanna. By not wavering from that focal point, they were able to plow a straight furrow. What "bandannas" do *you* have to keep on track?

Closely related to a sense of meaning and purpose are goals and plans. These are the natural outgrowth of our values, and help give direction and meaning to our experience. We human beings are unique in our ability to reflect and imagine. This ability creates the complexity of living in three dimensions: the past, the present, and the future. Our goals and plans, therefore, serve as a focus for our strivings and hopes and stimulate growth. Without them, we feel stagnant, anxious, and uncertain in a changing world.

For any of the recommendations in this book to make a real impact on your life, you should have some idea of what your values are. Implicit in my recommendations are many of my values, which I share with you. Among these are the values that life is good and we should live it to our fullest potential. I won't be so presumptuous as to tell you what all of your values should be; but it strikes me that being all that you are capable of being, in whatever circumstance you are in, is a good place to start. I also encourage you to make them strong enough to give you stability, large enough to give you a world view instead of a self-centered one, and flexible enough to grow with you as your understanding of the world grows.

I really like the old aphorism, "No wind blows well for a ship without a destination." In seafaring lore, a ship uses the light from the lighthouse to give it direction and keep it off the rocks and shoals. When the weather convulses in upheaval, the anchor is dropped to help it ride out the storm. In human terms, a sense of meaning and purpose is the beacon that guides our way, and self-esteem the anchor that helps us ride out the storms of stress in our life.

Stress Strategy #7

Developing positive self-esteem, and having a sense of meaning and purpose to your life will increase your resistance to stress.

Chapter Eight

Dealing with the "Force"

At first glance, "dealing with the Force" may look like something out of a *Star Wars* movie. But it's not. It simply refers to our original stress formula. Remember? F + R = S (Force plus Resistance equals Stress). To refresh your memory of the definitions of those terms, just use this paraphrase: Adjustment Demands (Force) + Inflexibility (Resistance) = The Wear and Tear of Life (Stress). In this formula, both Force and Resistance are Stressors, things that produce stress. Therefore, reducing either one of the stressors reduces the overall stress. In this section, we will discuss how to reduce the Force—adjustment demands—in your life in order to reduce stress.

We have already discussed the danger of too much change in a short period of time, such as a year. But it's not always possible to control the amount of change to which you are subjected. Alvin Toffler's popular book of a few years ago, *Future Shock*, impressively depicted the destructive consequences of our rapidly changing world. Today's immense technological advancements, the disturbing cultural shifts, the daily bombardment of vast amounts of information (most of which we can do nothing about), combined with the lack of stability in many of our previous sources of security such as the church and the home, all fuse to create a sense of impotence and threat.

To cope with this army of adjustment demands, you need an armament, an effective selection of tools that will reduce the demands to a manageable few. Life by the yard is hard, but life by the inch is a cinch.

Here are some methods of sorting through the multiplicity of demands that beset you, and turning them into a manageable number. These methods have the effect of channeling adjustment demands through a funnel so they reach you in a smaller, more orderly, and less frightening fashion.

1. Prioritize   "Does this *have* to be done?"

Adjustment demands have a way of "bullying" and intimidating you into feelings of passivity and helplessness. Sometimes, it seems that there are so many things that are screaming to be done that you feel overwhelmed. That's when you get Excedrin headache #32. Well, you can fight those bullies if you line them up and fight them one at a time. Trying to deal with them all at the same time is not only impossible, it's debilitating. Prioritizing serves the function of lining up your pressures, and putting those demands at the front of the line that are true priorities.

When you feel the pressure of multiple demands, pick them out one at a time and ask yourself, "Does this *have* to be done?" To prioritize, you must learn to make a distinction between what you *want* to do and what others *want* you to do—and what *has* to be done.

Every task can be divided into two parts: the bare-bones essentials of what has to be done and the multiple layers of expectations about how we would like to do it. The contemplation of what we would like to do and what others might like, coupled with the pressure of these frequently conflicting demands on our performance, can produce a paralysis of effort. We don't get anything done because we feel overwhelmed with the impossibility of our task.

Consider the person whose objective is to build a shelter before the storms arrive. The storms are due in a month. The basic requirement is relatively simple. The shelter only has to keep them warm and dry. Imagine, though, that their personal needs for status cause them to envision a structure requiring time and materials that turn their simple task into one requiring Herculean effort. While there is nothing intrinsically wrong with their desiring a mansion instead of a lean-to, it does change the level of pressure. It converts the simple objective of providing warmth and dryness in a month into a major source of stress.

In just that fashion, many people keep themselves under needless stress in their work by not separating the "have-to" components of their work from the "want-to" parts.

An accountant friend of mine had been looking drawn and haggard of late, and I asked him what was going on. He complained about his job, saying that there was just too much to do in too short a time. Being concerned about his condition, I asked him to explain in more detail what he meant. He told me that his boss had requested him to finish a financial report and have it on his desk by Monday. Added to this was the fact that he felt his job security was shaky and he couldn't afford to miss the deadline the boss had set for him. Monday was three days away, he didn't think he was going to make it, and the pressure was becoming unbearable.

Pressing the issue, I asked him if it were physically possible for him to finish the task, on time, when his boss first asked him for the report. "Of course," he told me. "The report only takes a couple of hours." "Well then, why have you been agonizing over it for several days?" I queried. He then went on to explain that this was a regular report and he had discovered a method of simplifying it. This would help the accounting department in the future and, he hoped, prove his value to the company. Developing the idea and getting it into the computer system was taking a lot of extra time and he was fearful he wouldn't finish on time. You might call it "turning a molehill into a mountain."

He went on to admit that this was something he did frequently and probably accounted for the chronic stress under which he labored. Placing himself under health-threatening stress over something he "wanted to do," he was on the verge of failing to do what he "had to do." It amounted to a self-fulfilling prophecy about losing his job.

When you are feeling stressed by the multiple demands of a job, strip the job down to its bare essentials and reduce the pressure you are placing on yourself. Deal with the additional layers of expectation only as you are able to handle them. This serves the purpose of "lining up" the task components with the highest priority items in front. By starting with the highest priority and accomplishing it, you can work your way through the other layers of expectation at your leisure, or not at all.

It will be helpful to you, in your efforts to manage stress, to discard some stress-creating myths. One myth is that if you work hard in an organized fashion, you will finish your tasks. Don't you believe it! You will never finish your tasks. There will always be more to do than you are capable of doing. By telling yourself that you can finish if you work effectively, you keep yourself under pressure.

The second myth is cousin to the first. In this myth, you believe that if you were a competent, capable, intelligent person, you would be able to do everything that needs to be done. Now you are really in a bind. If you don't deliver, your self-esteem goes down. With lowered self-esteem, your effectiveness is reduced and the problem compounds. Get rid of that kind of thinking. You'll be lucky to take care of your main priorities by working hard and diligently, let alone your lesser priorities. Besides, if you are intelligent, you will see more to be done and the pressure will never go away.

Think like this: "I will never get finished with all my tasks. I can only do what I can do. I'm going to concern myself with making sure that whatever I am doing is really a priority in my life. The rest can wait."

Pressure controls you only if you let it control you. Related to any task, there will usually be many more things we want to do— and others want us to do—than what we are able to do. So you can limp around feeling like a martyr to stress, or you can choose to step away from the pressure by prioritizing.

Prioritizing has a lot to do with values, of course, and it is expedient that you have a fairly clear picture of your values for this to be fruitful.

Make a list of the activities you engaged in during one week. Then add the number of hours spent on each activity. After that, make a list of things you consider to be values in your life. Now for the crucial test: Compare your weekly activities with the things you say are your values. Do they match? The results may be shocking. Some people place family very high on the list and watching television very low. Yet when they look at the results of this exercise, they find they spend more time watching TV than they do with their family.

How you spend your time is your business. Your values don't have to be my values; but if you spend most of your time on low-priority values, you will be under chronic stress and unfulfilled.

Once you have established a list of priorities, i.e., things that *have* to be done, then you're ready for the next question.

2. Delegate   "Do *I* have to do it?"

Once you have established your priorities—what *has* to be done, then ask yourself the next question: "Do *I* have to do it?"

There are many necessary tasks in this world, as well as in your life, that should be done. Something should be done about the danger of thermonuclear destruction, world hunger, and so forth. But if you let yourself feel responsible for everything in this world that should be done, you won't have any energy left to do what you, and you alone, must do.

To handle this stressful world, you not only have to be clear about what *has* to be done, but also what *you* have to do.

117

Some people run around in a stressful frenzy worrying about all the things they see that need to be done. In any complex endeavor, there are many tasks that need to be accomplished and these people elect themselves responsible. They have a condition I call "The Atlas Syndrome." They carry the world on their shoulders.

I see this manifested frequently in the corporate world. When I consult with industry, a common problem I find with managers is the failure to delegate. Some managers don't seem to understand what their job is. Managers aren't hired to *do* things; they're hired to *get* things done. A popular attitude with some managers is, "If you want something done right, you have to do it yourself." It is a destructive attitude, especially in the corporate setting. It overburdens its adherents with needless stress and prevents the development of staff resources.

I've heard managers say they would love to delegate but they can't. Their people are all incompetent and untrustworthy. Well, the manager who believes that should be fired! That belief constitutes a self-indictment. It is an admission of failure because the manager's job is to create and develop a staff who get things done. By saying they are no good, that manager has condemned his or her own efforts.

Failure to delegate is a mistake for several reasons: *1.* It creates unnecessary stress that will impair the effectiveness as well as the health of the manager; *2.* It prevents the development of staff resources; *3.* It diminishes the productivity of the organization.

You may think that this doesn't apply to you because you are not a manager. Think again. All of us are managers, because all of us have to make effective use of our resources to live successfully. That's management. The staff may be your children and the organization your family, but you're a manager. Learning to delegate applies whether you are delegating to your children, your husband or wife, your CPA, your physician, your repairman, your mechanic, your attorney, or your God! Get the picture?

Set your priorities, do what *you* have to do, and delegate the rest.

3. Compartmentalize   "Do I have to do it, *now?*"

Compartmentalizing is a marvelously effective cognitive technique for bringing adjustment demands under your control. Once you have Prioritized (Does this *have* to be done?) and Delegated (Do *I* have to do it?), then you are ready to subject the remaining adjustment demands to the question, "Do I have to do it *now?*"

Imagine that you are teaching a group of students in a classroom. The classroom is set up in the typical grid of row and column. Each student is sitting in his or her "compartment," called a desk.

Further imagine that every student in every "compartment" was yelling for your attention. Drive you crazy, right? No one could handle that kind of chaotic cacophony without soon coming to their wits' end.

You would probably react logically by yelling back, "Shut up! Now, one at a time!" Listening to, and dealing with, those students (adjustment demands) in their desks (compartments), one at a time, would be a manageable task. You could handle that without risking your sanity. You can't handle all of them at the same time, but you can handle all of them one at a time. Coping with that classroom has a parallel in life.

Prioritizing is similar to getting the students (adjustment demands) out of the room who didn't belong there; delegating is analogous to letting the janitor worry about cleaning the room; and compartmentalizing is keeping the students at their desks, talking to you one at a time.

Using these principles, you will distill your problems down to the ones you really have to deal with, and then line them up and knock them off one at a time. If you don't, you're going to make a monkey out of yourself.

THE EXECUTIVE MONKEY SYNDROME

Did you ever take Psychology 1A in college? If you did, you may remember a section that dealt with some research they called "the executive monkey experiment."

In this experiment, conducted at the Walter Reed Army Institute of Research, two monkeys were strapped into a contraption that permitted limited movement. Both monkeys had a little box in front of them on which there was a light and a button. The experimenters would turn the light on and then, within ten seconds, the monkeys would receive a jarring shock to their feet (researchers are not known for their commiserative tendencies). The button would forestall the shock if it were pushed within the ten-second "grace" period.

That would seem to be enough pressure by itself, but the researchers added an inventive twist. Only one of the buttons worked! The monkey whose button worked had the power to prevent both of them from being shocked if he pushed the button in time. Being responsible for the welfare of another, he was labeled "the executive monkey."

After twenty-three days of this pressure, the "executive monkey" expired without warning. An autopsy revealed the beginning of atherosclerosis (hardening of the arteries), kidneys that were well on their way to renal failure, and a perforated ulcer of the duodenum. The other monkey, not having the good sense to pass away, was sacrificed to the cause of science and was found to be without physiological abnormalities.

The moral of this story was supposed to be that executives are prone to stress-related diseases because they have responsibility for others. At first reasoning, that seems to make sense; and over-stressed executives the world over sympathized with that deduction.

That conclusion is not supported by this experiment, however; and the reason for choosing the term "executive monkey" is not immediately apparent.

Presumably, the so-called "executive monkey" was not burdened with any altruistic concern for the well-being of his fellow monkey. How could he have known his actions were benefitting another? He was simply acting in his own best interests. I doubt that he deliberated much over whether or not his actions helped another monkey. On the other hand, maybe that is the implication in using the label. I wonder who should be offended, executives or monkeys?

Also, there is a far more significant finding that developed from this research, although you won't find this in Psych 1A. In every other attempt to replicate (reproduce) this experiment, they could never get the same results. In every other instance, guess which monkey got the ulcer? That's right. The poor schmuck whose button didn't work. He knew he was going to get shocked when that light went on, but he was helpless to prevent it. It's called, "responsibility without authority" or, as it's known euphemistically in corporations, "mid-level management."

The most devastating type of stress is not heavy responsibility. It is having a sense of responsibility without the power to do anything about it! Responsibility won't kill you as long as your buttons work. But feeling responsible about something over which you have no control will send you to an early grave!

Let me give you an illustration using a situation I dealt with once. Read along and analyze the story for yourself. See if you can figure out why I said some of the strange things I said, before I explain them to you.

A woman, whom I shall call Mrs. Jones, made an appointment with my secretary to consult with me. The only information I had about her was from the data sheet (name, address, etc.) which the woman completed upon her arrival for the appointment. She came to the door. She was an attractive, well-groomed lady, but quivering like a bowl of Jello. Tears were ravaging her makeup as she appealed to me, "Put me in the hospital. I'm going crazy; please, put me in the hospital!"

She continued pleading with me to put her in the hospital with such incessant fervor that I couldn't get her to stop. Finally, in desperation, I said, "All right, I'll put you in the hospital." This served to calm her temporarily, and I quickly interjected that it

121

would be foolish for me to take her to the hospital until I at least knew what the problem was. She acquiesced to that logic and sat down. Trembling and weeping, she told me her story.

Her sixteen-year-old daughter had run away from home. She had been gone two weeks. Mrs. Jones had decided her daughter had probably set out across the country hitchhiking, as she had once threatened. With heart-rending laments she poured out her fears. "What if she's hungry?" "What if she's sick?" "What if she's hurt?" "What if she's been assaulted?" She continued with obsessive guilt. "What if I had spent more time with her?" "What if I hadn't been so strict?" Every "what if" intensified her quavering tearfulness.

"Mrs. Jones," I interrupted, "what is the worst thing you can imagine happening to your daughter? Is it that she would be picked up hitchhiking by some sex maniac who would rape her, torture her, kill her, and then throw her broken body in a ditch? And right now, as we talk, she is lying dead in some far away state?" "Oh yes," she gasped, "that's what I fear the most."

"Then let me ask you some questions. They may seem strange, but bear with me and try to answer them as best you can. If that happened, does it seem logical to you that eventually someone would discover her body?" "Yes," she acknowledged, "I believe they would." "If someone discovered her body, does it make sense that sooner or later, through dental charts or fingerprints, they would identify her?" She nodded her head. "And when they identified her, can you accept that someone would ultimately contact you?" Again, she agreed.

I then proceeded to systematically question her about how she would cope with each practical necessity that would eventuate from that contact. I insisted she respond to each query.

"They would ask you to come and identify the body. Would you go? How would you travel—by plane, train, car, or bus? Would you have the body flown back home for burial? Which mortuary would you choose? Would you have the body interred or cremated? What kind of funeral service would you have?"

I persisted in making her plan each detail, right down to the flowers she would choose for the funeral. I pressed her to decide on the minister, the church, the cemetery, and even the songs to be used at the service.

Finally, after about forty-five minutes of this seemingly morbid interrogation, I asked her, "Mrs. Jones, what has happened to your tears and trembling?" Self-consciously, she acknowledged, "I feel perfectly calm. I guess . . . I guess I don't have to go to the hospital after all." What a dramatic transformation! She looked better and felt better even though we had been explicitly discussing her worst fears. What does your analysis reveal as the reason for this reversal?

As long as she felt responsible for situations over which she had no control, she suffered severe stress. Feeling helpless over her daughter's possible condition had her on the verge of a nervous breakdown. She felt the need to protect someone who couldn't be protected. It wasn't in her compartment.

I pointed out to her that even though the prospect of her daughter's death was horrible, she had calmed down while talking about the aftermath. This was because she had begun to focus on what she *could* do, instead of what she couldn't do. If you insist on concentrating on the aspects of your anxieties, fears, or resentments you can do nothing about, you cannot avoid severe stress.

Remember this little stress organizer. *When you can't do what you want to do, do what you can do!*

Mrs. Jones wanted to save her daughter from harm. She couldn't. But she could plan how to deal with a specific possibility. When you want to do something but can't, look for something you can do, and do it. Don't make yourself impotent!

Worrying about all the things that might be happening to her daughter — something she wasn't sure was true, and couldn't control anyway — only gave her a sense of responsibility without authority. None of those "buttons" worked.

Planning on how to deal with the knowledge that her daughter had died was something she *could* do. She was capable of planning the funeral, dealing with the family, and preparing to get on with her life. Whether she wanted to or not, and whether she liked it or not, those were things over which she had control. They were "buttons" that worked.

For those of you dear readers who would worry, otherwise, nothing bad happened to the daughter. She did come home, and the family is reconciled.

At social gatherings, when people find out I am a psychotherapist, I am frequently asked, "How can you stand dealing with all those problems?" I give my standard response:

"I keep a clear distinction between what I want to do and what I can do; what is my responsibility and what is the patient's responsibility. I don't try to teach students who don't belong in my classroom. I know what I can do and what I can't do.

I *can* influence people when they are with me, but I can't control them when they are not. I *can* be the best therapist I know how to be, but it's up to them to be the best patient they know how to be."

I tell my patients, "I can give you the 'how to,' but it's your job to supply the 'want to.' "

When you are under pressure, you have a number of "students" wanting your attention, but you can only listen to them one at a time. When you are in one compartment, you can't worry about what is in another compartment.

For instance, when Mrs. Jones is in my consultation room for that hour, that is my compartment I don't think about Mr. Smith. I'm not in that compartment. I don't think about getting my car tuned up. I'm not in that compartment. I don't think about how my children are doing in school. I'm not in that compartment.

I'm in Mrs. Jones's compartment and it's the only one, at that time, over which I have any control. When Mrs. Jones goes home,

I am no longer in that compartment. I have no more influence and no more control, so I quit worrying about it. If Mrs. Jones calls me at three in the morning, I'm back in that compartment and she has all my attention because, once again, I have the potential for control and influence. I am not helpless.

The need to control one's environment is a basic psychological need. Having a sense of inner control is associated with better mental and physical health, higher self-esteem, and higher achievement. When elderly people in convalescent homes were given greater control over everyday decisions, they became happier, more alert, and had lower mortality rates than peers who were not given increased control. The feeling that external factors are in control of your life increases your vulnerability to stress.

When you focus your need for control on things that are "in your compartment," you minimize stress and maximize your mental health.

People get stressed when they can't find answers to their problems. It makes them feel that their life is out of control. Many times, it's because they are asking the wrong questions. The stressful questions are the ones that make you feel impotent. The question that gives you control is what I call "The Power Question."

If someone asks, "How can I get my husband to stop drinking?" that's the wrong question! That question leads to a feeling of helplessness. The Power Question is, "How can I live more successfully even though my husband drinks too much?" Trying to change the life of another person is not in your compartment. Changing your own life is within your control; changing someone else's is not.

Your husband's drinking is his compartment. Your living successfully is yours. You may *want* to help him stop drinking, but you are powerless if he chooses not to let you. So *put your energy where your power is* — in your own compartment, not his.

"How can I get my supervisor to treat me better?" Wrong question! Your supervisor's actions are not in your compartment.

Trying to come up with the answer to that question will put you under stress and leave you defeated. "How can I be happier and more successful on the job even though my supervisor doesn't treat me like I want him to?" That's the Power Question. That's the question that puts you back in charge of your life.

"How can I get people to respect me more?" Did you say to yourself, "Wrong question"? Great, you've got it. That question is unfruitful. The Power Question is, "How can I act so that I will respect *myself* more?" Questions concerning the conduct of others make you feel helpless. Their conduct is their compartment, and ultimately it must be their decision to change, not yours. Questions concerning what you are doing or need to do are Power Questions. Your conduct is your compartment and you can do something about that.

Asking the wrong question has only two possible results. It will leave you feeling vanquished and a failure, or you will become dominating and manipulative in a misguided effort to feel better about yourself by controlling everything around you. It doesn't work. One way makes you miserable, and the other makes everyone around you miserable.

It's okay to try to influence other people and situations— sometimes it works. None of what I am saying is intended to squelch your hopes and dreams. Life would be a lot easier if everyone around us would cooperate with our desires. If you can influence them, go for it. Just don't kid yourself about where the real power and the real success is. The real power is over what *you* do, think, and feel. If you concentrate your efforts on that, you will magnify your chances of success.

Sometimes, you feel you have done everything you can think of to be the best person you can possibly be in a dissatisfying situation. Despite what you feel are your best efforts, nothing changes and your life is stagnant. If you are in a situation where you have absolutely no ability to improve the quality of your life, get out! But don't be too quick to decide that that is the case.

You may merely be in the habit of concentrating on what you *want* to do, instead of what you *can* do.

There are occasions when if you spend your energy taking care of what *you* are responsible for, it helps others be more responsible. But even if it doesn't, your life will be improved by assuming responsibility for *your* compartment.

Stress Strategy #8

Only accept responsibility for
those stressors that have *to be*
done by you, *and that are*
in your compartment.
Then do them one at a time
in order of their priority.

Remember. Establish your priorities—what *has* to be done. Reduce those down to what *you* have to do—delegate. Then put the remaining tasks in compartments and take them one at a time.

If you follow that procedure, you can make molehills out of mountains.

Chapter Nine

Learning to Bend
So You Don't Break

The word reducing has the connotation of diets. Every time I look at the titles in the bookstore, it seems that another diet book is on the stands. Americans are quick to pounce on the latest easy method for losing weight. So, I have a diet for you also. This one reduces the weight of stress. The difference is that it is a mental diet and concerns what you put in your mind, not your body.

In the stress formula $F + R = S$, you learned that reducing the Forces (adjustment demands) in your life is one way to lower Stress. The other way is to reduce the Resistance part of the formula. There are two ways to reduce Resistance and lower Stress. One way is to replace rigid, stress-producing attitudes with flexible, resilient attitudes. The other method is to increase your level of competence.

REDUCING ATTITUDINAL RIGIDITY

The first way to reduce the Resistance part of the stress formula is to reduce attitudinal rigidity. If, as Socrates said, "The unexamined life is not worth living," then unexamined attitudes are not worth having. Adaptability, the cornerstone of coping success, requires flexible attitudes that permit growth and change.

Just as the computer-age acronym GIGO (Garbage In, Garbage Out) applies to what you feed your body, it also applies to what you feed your mind. You can't put "garbage" thoughts into your mind without producing "garbage" feelings and behavior. Or, as Old Testament wisdom put it, "As a man thinketh in his heart, so is he."

Since at least the time of this Old Testament proverb, there have been advocates of the belief that the quality of your thoughts is directly related to the quality of your life. It is most certainly related to your level of stress.

Like others who champion this position, I have observed a commonality of thought in those who live overstressed, unfulfilled, and unhappy lives. Albert Ellis has labeled these thoughts "irrationalisms." Almost all the patients I have ever had who suffered from stress have also been afflicted with at least one of these stress-inducing cognitions.

These cognitions, or "Mental Stressors," are usually unconscious and therefore elude awareness. It may be easier for others to discern these attitudes, reflected in your behavior, than it is for you to be aware of them. Their existence increases your vulnerability to stress, and they must be dealt with for lasting peace of mind.

To deal with them, you must 1. Acknowledge that they exist, 2. Be convinced that they are harming you, and 3. Determine to rid yourself of them.

The following four attitudes are the ones I have found to be most common. Each of them produces the rigidity of thought that increases stress.

1. I Must Be Perfect.
2. Everyone Must Love Me.
3. Why Does This Always Happen To Me?
4. I Can't Help It.

Examine your thoughts for one or more of these Mental Stressors and replace them with a Mental Flexor. In anatomy, a flexor is a muscle that enables a body to bend, so Mental Flexor is an apt description for an attitude that enables you to adapt.

MENTAL STRESSOR #1

I Must Be Perfect

If you are afflicted with this attitude, you are methodical, systematic, and exacting in your efforts. You are demanding of yourself and probably of others. The attention to detail and the effort you expend at your tasks is usually far more than the task requires. You subject each endeavor to minute scrutiny in order to detect the presence of any flaw or defect.

While this arduous procedure involves much unnecessary and tedious effort, it can lead to genuine attainment and accomplishment. Ah, but there's the rub or, in this case, the stress. Because, in spite of your achievements, you never let yourself feel lasting satisfaction. You are driven to do "still better" and to underrate and discount your achievements.

Since you seek perfection, you have defined the goal as the impossible; hence, you are destined to always feel the failure. And that's the killer. No matter what your accomplishments, you rob yourself of satisfaction and achievement by your unrealistic standards. Instead of feeling pride and contentment in your attainments, you feel defeat and frustration.

Using the classroom analogy, if you earn a "C," you berate yourself for not getting a "B." If you then receive a "B," you are unhappy because it was not an "A." When you finally achieve an "A," you condemn yourself for not getting it sooner. It is precisely

131

this sort of attitude that keeps you under constant tension and stress. Little wonder you are known as someone who can't relax.

In defense of your actions, you assert that you are a superior person, and conventional standards don't apply to you. In fact, your behavior is an overcompensation for the unconscious fear that you are not worthy of respect and acknowledgement. Your compulsive drive to do well is an unconscious attempt to disprove this nagging anxiety.

Prove that you are not a victim of your past, and loosen up with this Mental Flexor.

MENTAL FLEXOR #1

Improvement, not
perfection

Giving up the pursuit of perfection does not mean abandoning the pursuit of excellence. It simply incorporates satisfaction with achievement.

Life is a ladder. The process of growth and development is coincident with climbing the ladder of life. Each rung in the ladder represents a goal or accomplishment in life. Mr. and Ms. "I Must Be Perfect" make three mistakes regarding this ladder that keep them under stress.

Mistake #1. The ladder has a top

The first mistake perfectionists make is to assume that the ladder has an end to it. They think that some day, if they climb fast and hard enough, they will reach the top of the ladder and feel content. Believing this, they always measure their level of achievement by the rungs above them. As long as they see that there are more rungs above them, they continue their striving with the sense of failure and discontent.

In assessing their accomplishments, they feel that nothing is ever good enough. They always find something missing, or deficient, or that could have been improved. The implicit assumption is that a task can be done so perfectly it could not possibly be improved; and that is their goal. Until they accomplish that goal, they will permit no sense of success for fear it will reduce their motivation. Anything short of perfection opens them to charges of inadequacy, and their fear of being seen as inadequate or insignificant is so intense they compulsively strive for perfection.

Perfection is an illusion, because the ladder of life is infinite. There is no top to the ladder; it just keeps on climbing. Therefore, measuring your progress and your worth by the remaining rungs above you will always result in the stressful feelings of failure and hopelessness. Here's why: *There will always be more rungs above you than there are below you.*

Your assessment of progress is based on your frame of reference. When you first begin to develop, your frame of reference is small. That means your focus of comparison is limited. For instance, if you have never left your home, going to the store is a big trip!

Just as your world expands as you grow from infant to adult, so it is with achievement. Since, with each rung climbed, your frame of reference expands, your ladder increases in length with each accomplishment. To measure your achievement by the rungs above you is to always feel deficient. Each accomplishment puts the goal of perfection further out of reach because each accomplishment expands your awareness of what is possible.

I once had an insight into this process when I was attending university. I had the belief that knowledge was finite and, as I learned, I would reduce my ignorance. But the more I learned, the broader my frame of reference became, and I discovered so much more existed than I had previously thought. In trying to understand the world, I discovered worlds within worlds, and they seemed to never end. I wrote a poem describing my plight:

I used to think when I was young,

that the learning stage had just begun;

and that I would as time went by,

increase my knowledge to the sky;

but alack, alas, how wrong that goal,

for the older I get, the less I know.

It's amazing how ignorant I became between fifteen and forty. When I was fifteen, I thought I pretty much knew all there was to know. By the time I reached forty, it was clear to me that the world of knowledge was so vast I could never understand but a small portion of it. I felt ignorant by comparison. Since the world grows as you grow, if you judge your life by the achievements remaining above you, you have a problem.

Here's the solution. The only realistic measure of your progress is the number of rungs below you, not the number above. Don't ask yourself the question, "Have I arrived at where I should be?" That goal is perfection and, by definition, must lead to failure. Rather ask yourself the question, "Have I improved from where I was?"

The only thing that matters is where you are now, compared to your starting point—not where you think you should be.

Mistake #2. Everyone has the same ladder

The second erroneous assumption about the ladder of life is that it is the same for everyone. This causes perfectionists to compare their life with others and feel either superior or inferior. If they are higher on their ladder than another, they feel superior; if they are lower on their ladder than another, they feel inferior.

This leads to artificial rivalries, unnecessary competition, and the assessment of worth based on achievement.

Listen! Everyone has a different ladder. You do not know, as you gauge another's level of achievement, how far they have climbed to get there. Does a millionaire by inheritance have the same level of achievement as a self-made millionaire? Does an individual with a healthy personality who grew up in an intact, loving home demonstrate the same level of growth as a person with a healthy personality who came from a broken and chaotic home?

You can only compare your achievement with you. Comparison with others is misleading and counter-productive.

Mistake #3. All goals should be attained.

The third misassumption made by perfectionists is that goals (rungs) are the purpose of achievement. They regard goals as real things having value for their own sake, but with no other worth.

The "I Must Be Perfects" of this world are inwardly frightened of goals because they regard them as objects to be attained in order to indicate worth. Since their goal is perfection, they innately sense that its attainment, like the carrot in front of the donkey, is forever out of reach. Desire and anxiety intertwine, producing ambivalence. This ambivalence leads to the perfectionist's twin nemeses of indecision and procrastination.

With the perfectionist, the mere contemplation of a goal can precipitate feelings of failure and futility. Like the "Executive Monkey," the perfectionist feels the burden of responsibility (to prove his worth), but his buttons (achievement) simply don't work. The result is constant stress.

Goals, of course, are artificial creations whose primary value is to stimulate growth. The real purpose of a goal is not as something to be acquired, but as something to make us stretch and grow.

After all, the function of goals is just to keep us striving. It is in the striving that growth takes place, and *growth is the only achievement*. Those who have mastered the art of living understand that the journey is far more important than the destination.

By changing your concept of goals from that of goals as acquisitions to goals as stimuli for growth, you reduce their anxiety potential. See them as devices to make you stretch and develop, so that as long as you are improving, it is irrelevant whether or not you achieve all your goals. As Browning said, "A man's reach should exceed his grasp, or what's a heaven for?"

This mental adjustment will move the focus from the unattainable—perfection—to the attainable—improvement. The attitude of "I Must Be Perfect" results in feelings of impotence and failure, and stress! The attitude of "Improvement, Not Perfection" generates eager anticipation and the liberation of your potential.

MENTAL STRESSOR #2

Everyone Must Love Me

Feeling loved is a wonderful experience. Few would question that it may indeed be one of the most desirable of human experiences. However, to be enriching, the need for love must be appropriately balanced between what you give yourself and what you expect from others.

The victims of the "Everyone Must Love Me" attitude operate under the assumption that "What others think of me is more important than what I think of myself."

Believing this, these unfortunates govern their actions by what they believe is most likely to elicit the approval of others. They permit themselves to become dependent on others for the life-sustaining nourishment of acceptance. Speech, dress, beliefs, indeed all behaviors are monitored carefully in order to present to others the most "worthy-of-love" image possible.

The results of these efforts yield a personality that ranges from being well-liked, agreeable, gentle, and pleasant, to popular, extroverted, attractive, and sociable. They are frequently effervescent and enthusiastic. More than being merely sociable, they "market" their appeal to others. Their desire for praise is intense and compelling. They not only enjoy praise, they need it and seduce it.

Because of their mistaken attitude, they are especially vulnerable to the stress of separation, disapproval, and rejection. They require constant approval and affection and are hypersensitive to their absence. Deprived of adequate levels of support (and they need a lot), they are apt to feel worthless and alone. They become eager for the slightest display of approbation and, finding it, they manipulate its source for every drop available.

The stress experienced from separation, disapproval, and rejection is traumatic enough, but that is not the only danger. The constant vigilance they exercise in pursuit of their needs keeps them under steady pressure. Even when they are enjoying social success, they never lose a certain degree of tension in their personality.

For the "Everyone Must Love Me" devotee, the major cause of stress is the feeling of being powerless. We saw what devastation feelings of impotence and lack of control could generate in the "Executive Monkey" syndrome. In that syndrome, the feeling of impotence is caused by having responsibility without authority, or having buttons that don't work. The "Everyone Must Love Me" proponents face a similar dilemma. They feel the responsibility of winning the love of everyone, but they have no authority to control the love choices of others.

Erich Fromm once said that the degree to which we hate others is in direct proportion to the degree to which we hate ourselves. People who are filled with hate for others are actually indicating their own self-contempt. If that is true, and much research has borne out this wise observation, then its corollary is also true. The degree to which we love others is in direct proportion to the degree to which we love ourselves.

That means for someone to love you, they must love themselves. In order to love you all the time, they must love themselves all the time. See the problem? A person cannot give what they do not have. If your objective is to get someone to love you, then that requires they first love themselves. If you want them to love you all the time, they must love themselves all the time. Not very likely, is it?

Playing the "Everyone Must Love Me" game is tantamount to being on an emotional roller coaster. If you are with someone whose self-esteem lets them care about you, you're up. If you are with someone with low self-esteem — without much to give — you're down. It is impossible to have any security when you are requiring others to supply you with what you don't give yourself. You are asking them to do for you what they have enough trouble doing for themselves.

You can't always control how others feel about you, but you do have control over how you feel about yourself. Drop the Mental Stressor of "Everyone Must Love Me," and replace it with a Mental Flexor.

MENTAL FLEXOR #2

What others think of me
is important, but not as important as
what I think of myself.

With the belief "Everyone Must Love Me," you are implicitly saying that "What others think of me is more important than what I think of myself." That puts the control of your self-esteem in the hands of others.

Of all the significant ingredients of mental health and successful living, self-esteem may be the most vital. It services our need for nearness by making us feel worthy of intimacy and confident enough to risk it. To place that precious commodity in the unpredictable hands of someone else is to court disaster.

Don't ever put your self-esteem in the hands of someone else! They have enough trouble with their own, and it will leave you feeling helpless and stressed.

If you knew that you were going to have to live with someone the rest of your life, wouldn't you prefer it to be someone you liked, cared about, or even loved? More then anyone else you came into contact with, wouldn't you want to get along with this person above all?

Well, there is only one person you will have to live with the rest of your life.

It's not your mother or father. Even if you wanted to stay with your parents, it wouldn't be possible. In the natural course of time, you would grow up and move away or they would pass away. If you don't get along with your parents while they are living, you can avoid them. You don't have to live with them.

It's not your brothers and sisters either. If your relationship with them is troubled, you can move away or avoid them too. And it's not your friends. If friendships deteriorate, you can make new friends.

It's not even your spouse. In spite of vows to stay together, or the wish to stay together, divorce statistics make it abundantly clear that you don't have to live with a spouse the rest of your life.

As important as all these people may be, you don't *have* to live with them the rest of your life. If the relationships become intolerable, you can move away from them. But there is one person from whom you cannot move away; you cannot move away from yourself.

You have to live with yourself the rest of your life.

Doesn't it make sense that if you are going to get along well with anyone, you should start by getting along with yourself? Think about the way you treat yourself. If you treated your friends as poorly as you treat yourself, would you have any friends? If the answer concerns you, then change the focus of your efforts. Instead of spending your efforts in attempting to win the love and approval of others, consider winning your own love and approval first.

I can hear some people saying, "But that's being egotistical." It seems that some people live with the fear that liking and being proud of themselves will lead to selfishness. That couldn't be further from the truth. The selfish person has little concern for others, but he also has little regard for himself.

His selfishness is driven by the fear that he isn't worthy enough to deserve anything good, and he must grab it for himself if he is going to get it. He doesn't give much to others because he doesn't have much to give. A starving person doesn't have much motivation to feed others. A full stomach makes charity a simpler task.

By building self-esteem, you will not only reduce the stress that stems from being dependent on others for acceptance, but you will also be able to treat those around you better. It's a lot easier to give from a full bucket than an empty one.

Shifting the focus from what others think about you to what you think about yourself will put your self-esteem back where it belongs—in *your* hands.

This valuable truth has been distorted by some. Because it was so apparent that making other people's opinion of you more important than your own was disastrous to mental health, many helping professionals in the late sixties and early seventies went to the other extreme. Popular books and seminars touted the belief that what you thought about yourself was the only thing of importance. These "gurus" encouraged us to do whatever made us feel good, and if someone else didn't like it, it was their problem. This emphasis on "me first" was a good example of the pendulum swinging to the other extreme.

The issue is not resolved by choosing either polarity. While you cannot afford to make others responsible for what you alone are responsible for, you can't live as if you are on a desert island either. We live in a world of interdependence where social acceptance can be a key factor in personal validation. The rules of organized societies demand a respectful consideration of the rights and opinions of others.

You cannot manage the stress of interpersonal living by believing that "what others think of me is more important than what I think of myself." But you can't ignore what others think of you and manage stress successfully either.

Once again, a need for balance is demonstrated. Neither one of these opposing philosophies will lead to a reduction of stress. Instead, they both produce their own types of stress. A salutary balance between these beliefs is found in the mental flexor, "What other people think of me *is* important; it's just not *more* important than what I think of myself."

Here is a little tip that will pay rich dividends. I've even been so bold as to tell my patients that this one bit of advice alone will dramatically improve the quality of their lives. See what it will do for you. Live your life so that for each action you perform you could look in the mirror and say, "I respect you for doing that." If you can't say that, don't do it and don't let anyone make you. If you can say that, do it and don't let anyone stop you. Simple, huh? Well, not at first maybe; but it gets easier. Try it. You'll like it!

Seek the love, respect, and approval of others, but never at the expense of self-esteem.

MENTAL STRESSOR #3

Why Does This Always Happen To Me?

Tevye, the long-suffering poppa in the musical "Fiddler on the Roof," lamented to God, "I know that we are God's chosen people but, for once, couldn't you choose someone else?"

It's not difficult, at times, to feel that life is a laboratory and you have been singled out for a cruel experiment to find out how much suffering one human being can take. Life's experiences seem to run in cycles, and it may seem that yours have been in a down cycle longer than most. You may feel you have been discriminated against by getting more than "your share" of life's painful ordeals.

If these statements are true of you, the rest is predictable. You think of yourself as a victim, and tend to use phrases such as "not getting the breaks" or "having bad luck." Such is the need for the human mind to find meaning and purpose in life's events you may even go to the extreme of believing that you are being punished for some real or imagined transgression.

All of this puts you under considerable stress and increases your vulnerability to future stressful occurrences. The vehicle that accomplishes this is a feeling of helplessness. By convincing yourself that fate, luck, or an unkind deity is controlling your life, you provide fertile ground for the seeds of stress to produce a bountiful crop.

The feeling of being helpless or powerless in the presence of adjustment demands, or what I call "responsibility without authority," may be one of the most stressful feelings possible. It can literally kill you.

The treatment of prisoners of war during Korea and Vietnam was designed to convince the prisoners they had absolutely no control over their life. Punishment was frequently random and senseless, intended to show the prisoners that they existed at the whim of their captors. With identical treatment, some prisoners gave up and died while others survived. The survivors were able to avoid a complete feeling of helplessness by serving on escape committees, going on hunger strikes, planning sabotage operations, and other techniques which had the effect of giving them the sense they still had some control of their lives.

The debilitating feeling of helplessness likely to afflict you is not based on being a prisoner of war. It is based on the implicit assumption that your life is controlled by circumstances external to you such as fate, luck, or accident of birth. You may even give someone power over you and then submit to feelings of despair and powerlessness. But, "it ain't necessarily so." To paraphrase the Bard of Avon, "The responsibility lies not in your stars, but in yourself."

You may not have chosen to be in the situation you are in, but you have most certainly chosen your reaction to it. What happens to you isn't always your choice, but what you do about what happens to you *is* your choice.

The attitude of "Why does this always happen to me?" is a major contributor to stress. Believing that your happiness is determined by external sources produces a mental rigidity that denies you the ability to adjust and adapt to changing circumstances. You need to take immediate corrective action by changing to a more flexible way of thinking.

MENTAL FLEXOR #3

What happens to me is not what makes the difference. What I do about what happens to me is what makes the difference.

It may be that your neighbors and friends have fewer difficulties than you. They may have been wiser, or more fortunate, or they may simply conceal their problems better than you do. But that is their life, not yours. The only reality you have any control over is the one *you* are living, and to discourage yourself by bemoaning a supposed unfairness of fate is to dig yourself a deeper hole. What you need is not a deeper hole, you need a taller ladder.

Your situation could undoubtedly be improved; certainly your attitude toward it can be. Here's your ladder.

Part of the wisdom of the Bible states that "the rain falls on the just and the unjust alike." No one plants weeds; they just grow. And they grow in everyone's garden. They aren't put there to test you, they just are. Reality is similar. It can't be changed once it exists, and the issue before you is not "Why did this happen?" but "What am I going to do about what has happened?" Once again, asking the right question provides the best answer.

All of us know of stories where people seem to be cursed by an unjust fate. Yet, in spite of the tragedies that have befallen them, they remain cheerful, optimistic, and productive. They have every reason to be bitter, and yet, in many cases, they seem to be happier than less-afflicted individuals. That attitude didn't happen by accident. They achieved that result by concentrating their energies on what they were going to do about their situation, instead of what might have caused it.

You may be one of those people who doesn't believe that fate has caused your problems. In fact, you are certain that it hasn't because you know who has. Knowing that all consequences have antecedent causes, you have tracked down the causes of your distress, and they all spell Y - O - U.

You may even be proud of yourself for "owning up" to the fact that your misery is self-made. Poring over your past with a psychoanalytic microscope, you pick out each shortcoming and missed opportunity. You condemn and chastise yourself for all the things you should, or could, have done. But it doesn't give you much comfort, does it? And it doesn't change a single event.

It is possible, and even probable, that past errors have contributed to your present problems. So what? That's "last time," and the only thing you have any control over is "next time." The primary purpose for dissecting your past, other than morbid self-curiosity, is to understand it so you can deal with its effects.

Examine your past errors only with the intention of learning from them. As I tell my kids, "When is a mistake not a mistake? Answer? When you learn from it."

If condemning yourself for your past mistakes would make you a better person, I would be for it. But blaming and condemning doesn't change anyone. If it did, depressed people would be the best adjusted. They blame and condemn themselves all the time.

The Greek philosopher, Epictetus, wisely said, "To accuse others for one's own misfortunes is a sign of want of education; to accuse oneself shows that one's education has begun; to accuse neither oneself nor others shows that one's education is complete."

Therefore, to have the mental flexibility to withstand stressors, try this. Instead of thinking about *what* has happened to you, concentrate your energies on what you are going to *do* about what has happened. This will move you from the "passenger's" side of life's vehicle, where you feel helpless and guilty, back to the "driver's" side where you have control.

MENTAL STRESSOR #4

I Can't Help It

I am constantly amazed at how many otherwise capable people defend their self-defeating, counter-productive behavior with the plea that they are powerless. When confronted with their temper tantrums, aloofness, emotional coldness, and other inflictors of pain and distress, they throw up their hands and say the magic words of absolution, "I Can't Help It."

I'll never forget a patient who exemplified the worst features of the "I Can't Help It" attitude. I'll never forget him because the loss of his wife and family was so senseless and needless.

Edward C. came to see me at my request after I had been counseling his wife for several weeks. His wife had come to the painful decision to get a divorce. She could no longer live in a relationship without caring or communication. Ed didn't show any tenderness, shared nothing that was intimate and vulnerable, and didn't listen when his wife tried to share what she was feeling. His communication centered around either criticism and complaints, or giving lectures and advice. He had built distance between himself and his family, and none of them felt cared about or wanted.

After talking with Ed two or three times, it became obvious that he really did love his wife and had no desire for a divorce, but he also had no intention of changing his behavior. Knowing what was going to happen if he didn't change, and having accepted he had no interest in therapy to help him change, I tried one last time.

"Ed," I said, "you have told me that you love your wife, and I believe you're sincere. You have told me that you feel a divorce would destroy you, and I believe you mean that too."

I had his attention.

"Ed," I continued, "answer me this. Suppose you would touch your wife just once a day in some gentle, caring, tender, non-sexual way. Ed, you have told me that your wife is a fine wife and mother; suppose you would tell *her* that, or some other sincere compliment (he had a lot of good feelings for her), just once a day. And Ed, suppose you would, just once a day, ask your wife how her day went and then shut up and listen; don't give her advice or instruction, just shut up and listen. Ed, if you did these things, do you think you could save your marriage?"

Ed looked at me a little strangely and then said forcefully, "Of course! That's what she's been trying to get me to do!"

I confess that his answer surprised me just a little. Here was a man who wanted to save what he said was the most valuable thing in the world to him, knew how to save it, yet was doing nothing to save it. I had another question.

"Ed, since you have told me that you absolutely don't want a divorce, and you know that these changes would save your marriage, WHY DON'T YOU CHANGE?"

With firmness and finality, Ed answered me. "I can't help it; that's just the way I am."

What a tragic waste! Here was a man who was praised for increasing his competence on the job. If he needed a new skill to receive a promotion or raise, he would learn it. Yet he wouldn't make the effort to learn how to show the behavior that would save his marriage. He ended up losing all that was dear to him because his rigidity prevented him from making the changes that could have salvaged his future.

Does the "I Can't Help It" attitude produce stress? The human suffering I have witnessed as a result of this attitude shouts a resounding Y E S !

This rigid mental attitude produces tremendous vulnerability to stress because it prevents adjustment. The ability to make constructive accommodation to adjustment demands is the essence of stress-coping skills. If you tell yourself that you "can't help it," you are saying that you can't change. If you can't change in the presence of an adjustment demand, that means you have to resist, and that type of resistance skyrockets stress.

Aside from increasing stress, the inability to adjust precludes growth, and the lack of growth, as in a vicious cycle, produces another source of stress.

As indicated earlier, standing firm in the face of pressure can be a commendable virtue when you are defending a valued principle. But when it is merely rigidity in the service of false pride, it ceases to be commendable and becomes self-destructive. To curtail this possibility, try Mental Flexor #4.

MENTAL FLEXOR #4

*I wasn't born with
this behavior, I learned it.
If something I am doing
doesn't work, I can learn
something that does.*

Low self-esteem, poor social skills, lack of assertiveness, inability to express feelings, insensitivity, feelings of inferiority and unworthiness, guilt, fearfulness—these and many other characteristics limit the fulfillment of human potential. When you think of a little baby in a crib, remember this. That baby doesn't have a single one of these characteristics. If he or she is to develop them, they will have to be learned.

You were once that little baby in the crib. If you have any of these, or any other negative personality characteristics, you learned them. You weren't born with them and you don't have to keep them. Remember, if something you have learned isn't working, you can learn something that does.

If you have no skills for sharing your emotions and creating intimacy in your relationships, you can learn them. If you have not learned the social skills that would help you in your personal and business life, you can learn them. If you have learned to be defensive, you can learn to be open. If you have learned to be hostile, you can learn to be loving. This is one principle that doesn't suffer from too much repetition: "If what you are doing isn't working, you can learn something that does."

The world is full of books, classes, seminars, teachers, and therapists who would like to help you learn the skills that will increase your chances of success in life. No one is saying it is easy. It isn't. But I will bet if you do it, you will find it is easier than you thought it would be; and it is certainly rewarding. Life is better than death; fulfillment is better than emptiness; and both are worth the effort.

"Ah, but you can't teach an old dog new tricks," you say. "Yes, you can. If the old dog wants to learn them."

Call it naive and simplistic to believe that you can unlearn negative behavior patterns and learn new and more satisfying ones. Call it that, but consider the alternative and think again. All through my experience at working with change in people's lives, I have discovered that when people have the willingness to change, they usually find the power to do so.

Stress Strategy #9

Examine your attitudes for the presence of Mental Stressors, attitudes that make you Uptight, and change them to Mental Flexors, attitudes that make you All Right.

INCREASING YOUR COPING ALTERNATIVES

The second method of reducing Resistance is to increase the number of your coping alternatives. Resistance is increased when you are unwilling to change, and it is increased when you are unable to change. If your competence is limited, almost anything that happens to you becomes a stressor. *Anything that increases your competence increases your number of coping alternatives and reduces stress.*

When you are faced with a problem, and you have limited or non-existent coping skills for dealing with that problem, stress is increased. Lacking the flexibility for dealing with an adjustment demand increases Resistance, or rigidity, which increases stress. Like the Executive Monkey, you feel pressured to act, but powerless to do so.

As I indicated, people tend to feel that my job as a psychotherapist must be extremely stressful. They frequently ask me, "How can you stand to listen to all those problems; doesn't it overwhelm you?" I respond, "That's exactly what I say to my auto mechanic."

When I take my car to the mechanic, I feel helpless to understand what the problem is. My competence in auto mechanics is limited, so I can't deal with many of the problems that occur with my car. When I take it to the mechanic and tell him the symptoms, he says, "Oh, I know what the problem probably is. Leave it here and I'll have it ready for you at four o'clock."

Because he has the competence to understand and deal with the problem, he does not get upset or stressed by it. What would be a stressor to me is an occupation for him.

I love to speak in public. For many people, speaking in public would be a very stressful event. But because I am confident in my knowledge of the subject matter and confident in my speaking ability, it's not only not stressful, it's a delight. It's even a source of revenue.

Similarly, by building your competence in any area where you are experiencing stress, you will reduce the stress. If you are stressed in social settings, increase your social skills. If your job is stressful because of its difficulty, increase your job skills. If you are stressed because of an inability to make your feelings known to significant people in your life, learn better communication skills. Etc., etc., etc.

By increasing your level of competence in any stressful situation, you will increase the range of behavior for dealing with that situation. If you have a broad range of skills available for dealing with a problem, your chances of successfully resolving that problem are increased. That reduces stress.

Stress Strategy #10

Reduce stress in a situation by increasing your range of coping alternatives to that situation.

Chapter Ten

What to Do When the Horses Are Gone

Have you ever heard the expression, "Closing the barn door after the horses are out"? Well, so far, all we have talked about has been how to increase your resiliency to stress. The focus has been on building a stress-proof personality. That's important, but for some people it amounts to closing the barn door after the horses are out. If you are already under a great deal of stress, you don't need help closing the door; you need help finding the horses!

As in another old saying, "If you're up to your neck in alligators, it's easy to forget that your job was to drain the swamp!" If you are reading this book, the chances are that you are already experiencing stress and need help in dealing with its effects on you.

Later on, when you are stabilized, you can work on the other parts of the book and increase your resiliency to minimize the effects of stress. But for now, here are some emergency treatment measures that will give you immediate relief. Any one of these seven techniques will reduce the effects of stress; and the more techniques you use, the more benefit you will receive.

Stress Strategy #11

*Develop a set of stress-reducing
techniques for those times when it's too
late to prevent a stress reaction because
you are already experiencing it.*

1. RELAXATION

Relaxation acts as an antidote to the negative physical changes experienced under stress. The word relaxation as used in this context does not have its typical meaning. It is used here to describe a behavior which has the unique ability to change or alter physiological activity in a healthy direction. It is the physiological "other side of the coin" to stress. Among its major benefits is the altering, in a de-stressing direction, of heart and pulse rates, respiration, brain wave activity, hormonal levels, muscle tone, and blood pressure.

Relaxation techniques don't alter your situation or increase your stress resiliency permanently. They are a temporary reprieve from the punishing aspects of stress. Temporary or not, they are an important tool for you to add to your stress-coping resources.

Not All Relaxing Is Relaxation   Curiously enough, not everything we think is relaxing produces the physiological changes we have defined as relaxation. Taking it easy in the old rocking chair or sitting idly watching TV may be relaxing, but they don't produce the physiological changes that combat stress.

Herbert Benson, in his excellent treatise, *The Relaxation*

Response, documented the benefits and the nature of relaxation. To produce the physiological changes that de-stress the personality requires following specific procedures, which lead to what he has termed "the relaxation response."

There are several effective methods that contain the elements that elicit the relaxation response. Each has its adherents and its own unique value. I will briefly discuss these methods, then describe fully the procedure I recommend.

Transcendental Meditation   Much more popular a few years ago than it is now, TM, as it is known, does produce the relaxation response. The process involves meditating twice a day for twenty minutes. The meditation is accompanied by the repetition of a meaningless sound or word. This is called a mantra and is especially selected for the meditator by a teacher or "guru."

Describing the mantra as meaningless might be challenged by those who believe it to have an arcane, cosmic importance. To those less accepting, it appears to be simply a monosyllabic intonation.

TM has the disadvantage of being overlaid with a mystical aura which encourages an elitist arrogance in its disciples. It can also turn out to be quite expensive. Neither of these peripheral features of mysticism and expense is required to produce the relaxation response.

Yoga   Yoga is an Eastern philosophy originating in India. The complete philosophy is most intricate and esoteric, and its exotic Eastern concepts and vocabulary can seem farfetched to the Western mind.

Actually, there are several types of yoga, and one of them, more specifically a type called Hatha Yoga, has features which can be used effectively in dealing with stress. These features entail the adoption of various body positions combined with intricate breathing exercises.

The stress-reducing benefits are numerous including the additional benefit of increasing the body's flexibility. It isn't simple or quick, however, and requires a little more dedication than some people are willing to give.

Progressive Relaxation   Sometimes referred to as "deep muscle relaxation," this is a common and fairly popular method of relaxation developed by Edmund Jacobsen. The procedure requires that you alternately flex and then relax small muscle groups in your body. It is recommended that you do this sequentially, starting at your feet and ending with the muscles of your scalp and face. Hence, the name, progressive relaxation.

It is quick and easy with no unnecessary trappings. Its disadvantage is that it is too limited in scope. It fails to incorporate the benefits of mental imagery and breathing techniques which amplify the de-stressing qualities.

Autogenic Training   The word "autogenic" literally means "self-created." It consists of an intermixture of techniques including deep muscle relaxation, self-hypnosis, mental imagery, and meditation. It was developed by the German psychiatrist, Johannes Schultz, and advances some lofty ambitions. Highly structured and systematic, Autogenic Training proposes to lead the initiate into increasing levels of self-control. It is further contended that the level of self-control extends to the control of body functions, such that even disease processes can be altered.

While much of the hypothesis has a factual basis, its proponents are too evangelistic for my taste. Autogenic Training has some definite benefits, but it is tainted by the unrestrained, and frequently unsubstantiated, claims of its partisans.

Biofeedback   Biofeedback can be an effective electronic technique for monitoring and controlling certain body functions. The name aptly describes the method of operation. Biofeedback uses electronic apparatus to monitor biological functions and feed back the results to the user. For years, it was believed that some aspects of the body's operations were involuntary. In deference to this belief, the nervous system commanding these reactions was termed the "autonomic" nervous system. That assumption turns out to be not entirely correct.

We now know these responses, previously believed to be "involuntary," can be altered by conscious direction. You can use any of the techniques discussed in this chapter to affect that potential. But only biofeedback provides concrete, measurable evidence of the results of your efforts. Tangible proof of the efficacy of one's efforts allows most people far greater control and effectiveness.

What can you do? Biofeedback is used to reduce the tension associated with tension headaches, give relief to migraine sufferers, lower blood pressure in hypertensives, and reduce other stress-related disorders. The machines have no intrinsic therapeutic benefit. All they do is provide feedback as to the success of your efforts in altering selected body functions associated with stress.

There are biofeedback machines to measure muscle tension (the electromyograph or EMG machine), brain wave activity (the electroencephalagraph or EEG machine), electrical conductivity in the skin (the galvanic skin response or GSR machine), or those used to measure the temperature on the surface of the skin (temperature trainers). The latter machines are used effectively to treat migraine sufferers and Reynaud's phenomenon (unnaturally cold extremities).

One apparatus, the polygraph, combines three of these measuring devices, with mixed success, to detect truthfulness. You know it better as the "lie detector."

Self-Hypnosis   I have included self-hypnosis here only for purposes of explanation. I don't necessarily consider it to be a separate category because all of the techniques discussed can be defined as forms of self-hypnosis.

Let me clear up a few myths surrounding hypnosis. First, it has nothing to do with going to sleep. Originally, it was thought to be a sleep-like state, and the name hypnosis was coined from the Greek word *hypnos* (meaning sleep) to reflect that assumption. By the time it was discovered that it was not a sleep-like state, the public had already accepted the name hypnosis.

Hypnosis is a condition of increased alertness, a narrowed and selective awareness (intense concentration), and heightened suggestibility. The best definition of the phenomenon is: an altered state of consciousness.

Second, all hypnosis is self-hypnosis. The fallacy that someone can "put you under" against your will is fostered by the stage hypnotist, but has no basis in fact. Only *you* can permit yourself to have this experience, although you may not always be consciously aware you have done so. While it is true all hypnosis is self-hypnosis, it is also true you frequently enter this altered state without your conscious knowledge. Doubt it? If you have ever been watching television so intently that you didn't hear someone talking to you, you were in a mild hypnotic state.

Many things can produce this altered state of consciousness, including all the techniques previously mentioned. But the process is the same regardless of the induction technique. It involves a concentrated attentiveness to a communication; the communication is usually suggestive and can be verbal or non-verbal. The suggestions can also come from you or someone else. This is combined with an internal permission to accept the suggestions and allow your mind to engage in free-floating imagination stimulated by them. You can enter or leave this condition at will, and at no time are you out of control.

As these ingredients evolve, the beneficial effects associated with relaxation also occur. In addition, there is the potential for making positive life changes through the increased susceptibility to suggestion. Positive comments about one's self-esteem, or any other area of concern, have more impact in even a mild hypnotic state than in a normal state of consciousness. As with any form of learning, repetition increases the potential for retention.

The CALM Technique   I have designed The CALM Technique to be simple and effective. Since all the relaxation methods described do essentially the same thing, I prefer this method because it is the quickest and easiest to learn.

Incorporated into The CALM Technique are the best parts of all the other techniques. It has been scientifically constructed to produce the "relaxation response" and de-stress the personality.

This technique has been proven to relieve fatigue and help you cope with anxieties. It has been shown to relieve the stress that leads to high blood pressure, hardening of the arteries, heart attack, and stroke. It will even reduce the inclination to smoke, drink, or to "turn on" with drugs. It can also be used to help you sleep.

The CALM Technique will help conserve the body's store of energy, making you more alert so you can focus and concentrate on what's really important. Unlike drugs, it has no dangerous side effects. You can learn it in the privacy of your own home without needless mumbo jumbo or expense.

The word CALM is an acronym of the four essential components which evoke the relaxation response, making them easier to remember. Just follow the simple directions below, and practice until you have the process memorized.

Comfort

The first letter of the word CALM stands for Comfort.

Find a comfortable place and position, preferably where there is a quiet environment. While this might be a chair or any other place where you may sit comfortably, it *is* desirable to be in a sitting position. In a sitting position there is less tendency to fall asleep, and it has been demonstrated through research that there is a qualitative difference between sleep and the relaxation response. If you would like to use The CALM Technique as an aid in falling asleep, by all means lie down. However, if you are using it solely to obtain the "relaxation response," then remain seated for maximum benefit.

Adjust your body so that it is not in a "locked" position. In other words, avoid having your fingers intertwined or your arms and legs crossed. It is desirable to have your body in an open and receptive position for both physical and psychological reasons.

Attitude

The second letter of the word CALM stands for Attitude.

Relaxation is facilitated when your attitude is passive and non-achieving. *Relaxation is not something to attain; it is something to permit.*

A simple mental technique that will help you acquire this attitude of constructive passivity is to say "So what?" to any distracting thought or idea. When the thought occurs, "I wonder if I'm doing this right?" the response is, "So What?" If you think, "I wonder if I'm getting the desired results?" the answer is, "So What?" Whatever the thought is that would distract you, counter it with, "So What?"

Do not allow yourself to work hard at "trying" to relax. The idea is to have a passive, non-achieving attitude that will allow you to slide into the relaxation response.

Letting Go

The third letter of the word CALM stands for Letting Go, and refers to the relaxation of muscle tension. Tense and tighten the muscles of your body, starting with the feet. Moving in large muscle groups, continue sequentially up to your scalp and face. Hold the tension in the muscles for a few seconds and then relax. Repeat that for each muscle group. When every muscle group has been tensed and relaxed, remain relatively motionless. Mentally scan your body, checking all of your muscles and simply say to yourself, "Relax." Allow all of your muscles to become limp and heavy.

Any one of several techniques will assist you in the process. One that will be instrumental in achieving this result is to imagine yourself in a "hot tub," soaking away all of the cares of the day, each muscle becoming limp and relaxed. The more vividly you can see that scene, the more deeply relaxed you will become.

Another technique is to pay attention to the muscles in your jaw. People in occupations that involve sustained mental activity have a tendency to store up tension in their jaw. While concentrating heavily, without knowing it, they clench their teeth, producing muscle tension in the temples of the head. If you will put your fingers in that area, and then clench your teeth together, you can feel the muscles tighten up and produce tension in the face and jaw. Over the course of a day, it can lead to a pretty good tension headache. Some people even do this to the extreme of grinding their teeth at night, a practice known as bruxism. Aside from being a potential dental problem, it is ususally evidence of considerable tension.

To relax this tension, allow your teeth to part slightly, keep your lips together lightly, and allow the jaw to sag. Imagine that if the muscles were not holding the jaw, the jaw would fall off. Feel the relaxation.

If you suffer from bruxism, or have tension headaches, don't limit this relaxation of the jaw to the times you engage in The CALM Technique. Monitor the tension in your jaw several times a day and then concentrate on relaxing it.

Another method designed to help you let go of all muscle tension is to relax the muscle in the forehead. This muscle, the *frontalis* muscle, is the most tension-sensitive muscle in the body. If there is muscle tension anywhere in the body, but particularly the upper torso, the tension will be reflected in the *frontalis* muscle. Conversely, concentrating on relaxing this muscle tends to relax the rest of the body.

Relaxing this muscle can be accomplished by imagining a warm hand (it's your fantasy, so make it any hand you want) gently stroking your forehead. Allow the muscles of the forehead and the scalp to sag and relax.

In summary then, relax all the muscles of the body by vividly imagining you are in a "hot tub" and all of your muscles are becoming limp and heavy. Picture each muscle as limp spaghetti that has been boiled too long. Allow the muscles in the jaw to relax by letting the teeth part slightly and the jaw sag, and picture a warm hand soothing your forehead.

Even when you feel deeply relaxed, you can find a way to relax even further.

Mental Focus

The final letter of the word CALM stands for Mental Focus. This Mental Focus, perhaps the most important part of The CALM Technique, is the essential ingredient in producing the relaxation response.

A concentrated mental focus can be created by making a blue dot on a piece of white paper (if this isn't possible, just close your eyes, but the blue dot has an additional benefit described later). Stare at the blue dot and begin counting backward from 100 down to 0. The method for counting backward is as follows: "think" the number in your mind, e.g., 100, as you inhale, and as you exhale, think the word "calm."

Allow the word calm to be drawn out to parallel the length of the exhalation. For example, as you inhale, think the number; then as you exhale, think "calmmm." As you inhale, think the number, e.g., 99; then as you exhale, think the word "calmmmm." Repeat this procedure all the way down to zero.

At all times, allow the counting to correspond to the natural rhythm of your breathing. Allow the rib cage to collapse normally, producing a slow, gentle progression into deeper and deeper relaxation. As you exhale, notice how your body feels heavier and more relaxed than when you inhale. By gently prolonging the amount of time you exhale, you can progressively deepen the relaxation response.

As you count backward, deepening your comfort, you may find your mind beginning to wander, and you forget which number you were on. Remember how to handle that? If you discover your mind has drifted, your attitude is, "So What?" Pick a number that was in the general area you remember and continue. If you never get to zero, "So What?" You are progressing to relaxation, not zero.

When and if you do reach zero, or at whatever time you decide to quit, a word of caution is warranted. Your body will be deeply relaxed and your blood pressure will be lowered. In this hypotensive condition, you should not jump to your feet or engage in anything strenuous. Give yourself time to readjust to a state of readiness before you resume normal activity.

Completing The CALM Technique will take from 12 to 15 minutes. You will derive much benefit if you practice it at least once a day. If you are under abnormally heavy stress, do it two or three times a day.

Now, here's where the "blue dot" enters the picture. Put a smaller version of the blue dot somewhere you look periodically. I recommend putting it on your wristwatch or calendar. Both are places associated with timetables and pressure. Every time you look at your watch or calendar, it will, by conditioning, calm you down.

After you have practiced The CALM Technique for a few weeks, you will discover what I call "the eye of the storm" phenomenon. While things are in turmoil all around you, you will be able to produce the relaxation response by merely looking at the blue dot and thinking the word "Calm." Even though there is a storm around you, you will be in "the eye of the storm," calm and serene.

2. EXERCISE

The role of exercise in creating a more stress-resistant body has already been discussed. But exercise does more than help you become stress-resistant. It also reduces some of the negative effects of accumulated stress.

Stress is experienced partly as a feeling of tension. This is true because, under stress, both your mind and your body become rigid as they attempt to deal with the stress reaction.

Physically, muscles tense for action in subliminal preparation for action. Under prolonged stress, the muscles remain tense and the body reflects this tightness in posture and movement. Chronically tense people have muscles similar to emotional armor plating.

163

When a muscle is tensed, tiny lactic acid crystals accumulate in the muscle tissue, creating discomfort in the muscles. You have probably felt a soreness in your muscles the day after a strenuous workout. With sustained tension, your muscles, in time, will become stiff and sore just as if you have had a workout.

People who have much experience in exercising understand muscle stiffness and soreness very well. They also know that the best way to reduce that soreness is to exercise some more. The stretching, movement, and body heat that are a part of exercise can eliminate muscle soreness.

The tension and muscle soreness of stress can also be alleviated by exercise. The second benefit of exercise in reducing the effects of stress is biochemical. Recent discoveries have revealed the brain's ability to secrete a chemical that is virtually identical to morphine. The name for this chemical reflects this relationship. It is called "endorphin," meaning "the morphine within." Like morphine, endorphin acts as an analgesic for pain and a mood-elevater. That means while it is taking away your aches and pains, it is also elevating your mood, making you feel happier.

Marathon runners are familiar with a phenomenon known as "hitting the wall." About two-thirds of the way into a twenty-six-mile marathon, runners report a sensation they describe as "hitting a wall." The feeling is one of complete fatigue and an inability to continue. However, if they do find the will to continue, they "break through" the wall into a state of euphoria, painlessness, and renewed endurance. They feel as if they could run forever.

Exercise physiologists now understand the reason for this phenomenon. At the moment of "breaking through the wall," the brain secretes a massive injection of endorphin. The effect is as if the runners have received a large injection of morphine, eliminating their pain and giving them an increased sense of well-being and endurance.

While the phenomenon of "breaking through the wall" is the result of the extreme body stress caused by strenuous exertion, endorphin is secreted in lesser amounts at even moderate levels of exercise.

For years, I was proud of a reputation I had as a psychotherapist who was especially good with depressed patients. Whenever I treated someone who was depressed, I always insisted that aside from their "talk therapy," they must engage in regular, moderate exercise. That usually meant I got them to walk a mile or two every day.

I didn't have any profound scientific reason for requiring the exercise other than my belief that one should treat the whole person. With a few qualifications, I accept the idea of "sound body, sound mind." Basically, I thought if they were feeling better physically, it would be easier to treat their depression.

I almost always had a high success rate which I, of course, attributed to my skill as a "talk" therapist. While I hate to give up the idea that it was my skill as a therapist that achieved the results, I now have to acknowledge that at least part of the benefit was derived from the exercise.

Getting my patients to exercise was like giving them a daily shot of morphine. The endorphin secretions caused by the exercise acted as a powerful anti-depressant.

A word of caution must always be voiced when exercise is recommended. Exercise stresses your body by making demands upon it. This type of stress can be very beneficial, or very detrimental if you do not pair the level of activity to the body's capacity and limitations. High amounts of sudden, acute physical stress can devastate an unadaptable body. The same thing happens if the stress is psychological. In both cases, whether the stress is physical or psychological, it is important to slowly and progressively increase your competence and flexibility. This method increases your tolerance to, and recovery from, stress.

It is advised that people over a certain age, usually thirty-five, consult with a physician before they begin an exercise program. I think everyone, regardless of age, should do so. You may be athletic and young but not aware of an inherited potential for a possibly life-threatening reaction to certain types of exercise. Make sure you visit a physician who is knowledgeable about exercise. Many aren't.

If you want to make your body more stress-resistant, exercise. If you want to reduce the negative effects of stress, exercise. The benefits of regular, moderate exercise are simply too well documented for any health-conscious person to ignore.

3. VENTILATION

The word "ventilation" refers to the process of eliminating mental and emotional waste products from the mind. It is known clinically as verbal catharsis. You can think of it as a laxative for emotional constipation.

In the normal course of living, your body builds up waste products which must be regularly excreted if you intend to stay healthy. You know this, and you make allowances for it in your everyday activities. As a matter of fact, if anything interferes with the regular elimination of your body's waste products, you become concerned. Some pharmaceutical companies make a pretty good income catering to these concerns.

But did you know that the mind builds up waste products too?

These are emotional waste products and they need to be excreted just as certainly and as regularly as your body's waste products. Stress can cause "emotional constipation." Especially in men.

Men, in most cultures, are encouraged to "be strong" and to avoid anything which would contradict the image of strength. This usually means the suppression and repression of emotions viewed as weak. Humiliation, shame, embarrassment, sorrow, and other normal emotions are denied expression by this unwritten law of "machoism." Women, in contrast, are accepted for expressing their feelings freely and being vulnerable. They usually create supportive friends with whom they share their feelings. It is documented that women seek therapy far more than do men. Men don't go to therapy; they just commit suicide at twice the rate of women. Women talk out their feelings and live; men don't and die. In my opinion, the inability to express problem feelings is also a partial explanation for the higher mortality rate for men.

Whenever you experience *any* emotions, but especially negative ones, an emotional residue is created which needs to be excreted. Refusing to talk about your feelings isolates you. Human beings simply don't function well in isolation, and the self-imposed isolation of emotional repression is teeming with negative side effects.

Without the reality check that shared feelings provide, thoughts and perceptions can become distorted. These distorted thoughts and perceptions lead to further distortions which can provide fuel to psychotic tendencies. The waste products of emotional repression produce a stench that permeates the mind.

It also precludes bonding—that attachment we make to significant others that not only humanizes but enriches our lives. Holding feelings in isolation multiplies the fear of rejection which is its progenitor. The more we isolate ourselves emotionally from others, the greater our vulnerability to stress.

The role emotional repression plays in psychosomatic illness is well documented. Like energy, emotions cannot be destroyed. The need for expression remains, and repressed emotions can be displaced through the organs of the body. Combined with the unhealthy repercussions from chronic muscle tension, there is evidence that repressed emotions produce noxious biochemical changes which can jeopardize health.

It's fascinating to learn that the chemicals contained in the tears produced from onion juice are chemically different than the tears secreted because of emotions. Interesting, huh?

Could it be that undesirable biochemicals are created by negative emotions, and they need to be excreted? Could it be the body uses the mechanism of tears as one way of ridding the body of these chemicals? Would that explain why you frequently feel better after a good cry? Makes sense, doesn't it? The evidence would appear to support this theory.

People are the only "animals" definitely known to shed emotional tears. Studies at the St. Paul-Ramsey Medical Center by a research team under the leadership of Dr. William Frey have suggested that emotional tears rid the body of toxins which accumulate under stress.

Once again, men are denied this outlet by a belief system ridiculing the "weakness" of crying. It may be that we should all become more comfortable with the need to cry, and not hold back those tears.

But another type of "excreting" is not equivocal. The need to talk out our feelings is essential to dealing with stress. Whenever we feel such emotions as shame, anger, fear, humiliation, embarrassment, or any vulnerable feeling, we need to release those emotions verbally. Nothing else will suffice.

Expressing an action based on the feeling is not the same as expressing the feeling. Verbally attacking someone is not the equivalent of verbalizing your anger. Blushing is not the same as saying you are embarrassed. The feeling itself needs to be articulated, not just expressed through an action prompted by the feeling.

A man came to see me, reluctantly, on recommendation of his physician. He had a history of ulcers and had recently developed a bleeding ulcer that was threatening to perforate. Aside from the physical intervention he was providing, his doctor felt the man needed to address some psychological issues in order to have a lasting recovery.

The man was the strong, silent type, so admired in movie westerns. His history was replete with reasons for strong emotion, but he prided himself on keeping an implacable façade. As far as anyone else knew, nothing ever bothered this man. Throughout his troubled childhood, his rocky marriage, and his beleaguered job history, he boasted that he just "sucked it up" and kept a calm exterior. "Spilling your guts about your problems," he informed me, was for "sissies and women," and a real man dealt with his problems within himself. "Even as a child, I refused to cry when spanked," he blustered.

Here was a man whose philosophy of problem-solving was literally killing him, but he was determined to continue it.

I wanted to persuade him his emotional repression was unhealthy. I explained to him that repressing one's emotions made one weaker, not stronger. "Look at your history of ulcers," I charged. "You simply can't keep holding back your feelings and fully recover. You've got to talk to someone."

Partially convinced but still wary, he challenged: "Well, who am I going to talk to?" "You could talk to a therapist, like me," I offered. "I came to you this once because I had to," he retorted. "I'm not coming back. You guys are too expensive and, besides, you 'shrinks' are more screwed up than I am."

Not interested in debating the subject, I countered, "Then talk to a trusted friend." "I don't have any close friends, never have," he protested. Pretty certain of his response, I nonetheless suggested, "Talk to your wife." "Are you kidding?" he laughed. "She's the last person I'd talk to about my problems. She'd never let me forget it." Caught up in an almost perverse obstinacy, I tendered, "How about a priest or minister?" Not surprisingly, he demurred, "What do those people know about life? And don't suggest talking to God; I'm not religious."

By now, it was becoming clear, even to him, that he had a pathological need to avoid exposing his feelings. It kept him distant and apart from loved ones, robbed him of potentially fulfilling intimacy, and menaced his very life.

Aware that he was finally beginning to understand, I pressed home the point. "Do you have a tape recorder?" I asked. When he answered that he did, I exclaimed, "Then talk to *it!*" I told him he didn't have to listen to what he recorded, but he did have to verbally discharge his repressed feelings.

He finally got the point, and I hope you do too. Talking out thoughts and feelings is a crucial method of preventing the harmful byproducts of emotional repression. For full benefit, all feelings, whether positive or negative, need to be shared. Expressing negative feelings alone has merit, but expressing positive feelings adds the advantage of strengthening our loving attachments. And that's the best stress reduction of all.

4. ESCAPE

"I can't take any more of this stress; I've just got to get away somewhere this weekend." How many times have you said that to yourself? Getting away from our problems, even for a little bit, can provide the space to reorganize our energies and re-establish our motivation to cope with an overstressed life.

Escaping to another atmosphere helps us to temporarily divert our minds from the tasks and mental burdens that are producing our stress. I like to think of them as Stress Vacations.

The "escape" doesn't have to be physical to be effective. Mental escapes can be just as beneficial. To qualify as an escape, it must simply be something that has the ability to divert our thoughts from stressors without adding additional burdens.

A word of warning about "escapes" is warranted here. An activity engaged in to *avoid* your problems is not a stress-reducing escape. A Stress Vacation has as its purpose the marshalling of our resources in order to cope more effectively with stressors. The implicit intention of a Stress Vacation is always to get back to the fight, but with renewed energy and commitment.

A physical escape can be as simple as a walk in the park during lunch hour, or as complicated as a vacation to an exotic spot. Mental escapes can be as plebeian as watching television, reading an engrossing book, or working on a jigsaw or crossword puzzle.

Whatever it is, it must have the power to completely divert our minds from stressors. It's not an escape if you can take your problems with you.

5. CREATIVITY

Closely allied with the concept of "escape" is that of engaging in creative activities to combat stress. Creative endeavors combine the benefits of mental diversion with a feeling of accomplishment. The additional virtue of a sense of productivity adds the advantage of enhanced self-esteem to this form of diversion.

Any type of enterprise such as needlepoint, painting, playing a musical instrument, building models, singing, or gardening can fulfill the requirements for this delightful stress-reducing tactic.

While it is important for the venture be creative and diverting, it isn't necessary to be good at it. As long as you enjoy it, the benefits will accrue. Remember, the mechanism by which creative activities reduce stress is mental diversion, enjoyment, and a sense of accomplishment. If you apply perfectionistic standards to your creative activity, you will negate the benefit. Don't turn your stress-reducing efforts into an achievement-driven pressure cooker.

6. EMOTIONAL NOURISHMENT

Just as your body has to be well fed to function optimally, so does your personality. Emotional nourishment refers to measures I like to characterize as "soul food."

What is emotionally nourishing to one person may not be to another, so it's difficult to draw up a list of emotionally nourishing exercises. But here are some things I find to be food for my soul. Perhaps they will give you an idea of what I'm talking about, and you can look into your own life for similar examples of "soul food."

171

A few years ago, when I was working full-time as well as being a full-time graduate student, the days were quite long and tiring. When I came home from an especially taxing day, usually late in the evening, my family would already be in bed. Before I went to bed, I would groggily totter into my daughter's room and observe her sleeping in her crib.

For long minutes, I would stand quietly and look at my little baby girl with her long, soft eyelashes lying gently on her alabaster cheeks. A subtle tranquilness would begin to suffuse me and I felt my tension unwinding with the steady rhythm of her peaceful breathing. The small perfection of her body, the little curls of her sleep-tousled hair falling across her forehead, the sense of wonder that I had a part in creating this miracle, all combined to soothe and sedate my agitated spirit. After several minutes of this "soul food," I would go to bed and fall contentedly asleep.

Here's another example.

Sometimes my wife and I will sit in front of the fireplace in the evening with a bottle of champagne. We'll just look into each other's eyes, talk, and sip champagne. The evening will glide blissfully along with time being irrelevant. The talk will drift— the past, the present, the future—and then back again. The layers of restraint and inhibition melt away in the glow of the fire, and we share little thoughts and feelings that seem meaningless by themselves but, in this atmosphere, create a deeper sense of intimacy and attachment.

These special moments almost always develop spontaneously, but they invariably produce an experience that fills the heart and enriches the spirit. (Sometimes we will do the same thing in our Jacuzzi tub with bubble bath. We call it our "double bubbles" time.)

Or the nourishment might come on a warm summer evening, as I walk along in contemplation. Sometimes I can look up and it seems the sky is a huge piece of black velvet and someone has sprinkled a handful of diamonds on it. As I stand there under the glittering stars and sense the vastness of the universe, I feel a transcendence to my soul. I feel a oneness with my Creator, and a profound, stirring exultation engulfs me.

A person's values create their sources of nourishment, of course, and what is nourishing for me may not necessarily be nourishing for you. But I think you get the idea.

It's one thing to be *fed,* but it's something else to be *nourished.* When you are under stress, you need sources of nourishment. Think about those experiences that have left you enriched and better than you were. Seek them out. Cultivate them. Then, when you are under stress, find ways to bring them into your life regularly.

7. LAUGHTER

We are just beginning to understand the wisdom of the proverb, "A merry heart doeth good like a medicine. . . ." Laughter is not only fun, it's therapeutic. If you are one of those solemn types who regards laughter as frivolous, do yourself a favor and read *The Anatomy of an Illness,* by Norman Cousins.

Norman Cousins, the former editor of the *Saturday Review,* was diagnosed as having ankylosing spondylitis. Medical science isn't completely sure what it is, let alone how to cure it. They only know it is always fatal.

He recounts in the book how he lay in the hospital bed, passively waiting to die. It eventually occurred to this normally assertive man that, if the physicians weren't even sure what the illness was, it was foolish to lie there waiting to die. He decided to fight, but he didn't know what to do.

He developed the belief that having affirmative emotions could enhance his body chemistry and aid healing. Feeling that he already had hope, love, and faith, he decided to add laughter.

Determined to experiment, he had amusing movies, such as Candid Camera and the Marx Brothers, brought to his room. He demanded that no one visit him with a sad appearance. He wanted his day to be filled with jokes, funny movies, and comedy records. Sometimes he would have the nurse read to him from humorous books. He wanted to fill his day with laughter.

He made the joyous discovery that an especially hearty period of laughter had an anesthetic effect and would give him at least two hours of pain-free sleep. He wondered if he could continue that trend if he increased his opportunities to laugh.

Tests of sedimentation rates indicated improvement after a period of laughter. The improvement lasted and was cumulative.

It worked. Soon, other patients were wandering down the hall to his room to see what all the guffaws were about. The hospital staff informed him that he would have to stop his activities because it was disrupting hospital routine.

Cousins soon decided the worst place for him to try to get well was in a hospital.

He went home, against medical advice, and in time completely recovered. He is alive and well today. A living testimony to the therapeutic powers of laughter.

None of this tribute to laughter is a recommendation to discontinue medical treatment. If you are ill, follow your doctor's advice. Just don't ignore the healthful advantage of laughter. Laughter produces salutary changes in body chemistry which facilitate healing and recovery. So, especially when you are under stress, fight back with a good belly laugh.

You don't really need outside sources to cause you to laugh, you know. The best source may be you.

For some time, I had a reputation as an "expert" in child psychology. I wasn't always sure I deserved it, but it did stroke my ego and I enjoyed the attention. One night, after a particularly hard day, I went into the room of my oldest son. He was about nine at the time. I had been trying for weeks to effect a change in the way that he cleaned his room—or rather, in the way he didn't clean his room!

I tried everything, or so it seemed, with no success. This particular night, I was fed up and out of control. In a short time, I was aware of myself standing over this nine-year-old boy cowering on the floor, shaking my finger in his face and yelling threats. He was really frightened.

Divine providence must have intervened because I saw myself as though I was watching another person. What I saw was a large adult man, so-called expert in child psychology, scaring the wits out of a little boy with intimidation and threats. Not a flattering picture.

It occurred to me it would be really funny if someone video-taped the whole scene and played it behind me the next time I was pontificating at one of my child-raising seminars.

I started to laugh. I couldn't stop. I fell over on his bed, convulsing. *Now my son was really scared!* He probably con-cluded his old man had finally flipped out. When I did regain my composure, I knelt in front of him and did something I seem to have to do a lot. I asked forgiveness.

I said, "Son, I want you to know what happened wasn't your fault. I don't like your room to be dirty, but you didn't deserve all that anger. That was Daddy's problem; you didn't cause it. Will you forgive me?"

You know, children are a lot like dogs. You can kick a dog in anger and he will run away in fear; but if you call to him with a soft, loving voice, he will come back to you wagging his tail to get his ears scratched.

When I asked my son to forgive me, a big smile creased his tearful face. He threw his arms open to me and said, "It's all right, Dad. I forgive you." We held each other tightly. Now it was my turn to cry.

What a great experience! I enjoyed laughter and emotional nourishment at the same time, and my son received an example of what an adult should do when he makes a fool of himself.

It's a healthy practice to be able to see the absurdity of some of life's tribulations, and chuckle them into perspective. After all, life is simply too important to take it so seriously.

Chapter 11

The "PEP" Zone

There are people—you may be one of them—who have longed for a stress-free environment. They dream of basking in the sun with nothing to do, or even to think of doing. No demands, no pressures, no conflicts; in short, nothing to adapt or adjust to. Sound perfect? Seem too good to be true? Well, the research seems to indicate it may very well be too good to be true.

The problem of stress presents a curious paradox. Too much of it can lead to all the different psychological and physical disorders known collectively as "distress." Yet, too little stress can be damaging also.

The human brain apparently requires a certain level of stress to function properly. It wasn't designed to do nothing and it does nothing very poorly.

Research has been carried out using deprivation tanks. A deprivation tank is a device purporting to eliminate all sensory input to the brain. Volunteers in the research were blindfolded, had their ears plugged, and were suspended motionless in an enclosed tank of water heated to their exact body temperature.

While the eradication of all stimulation was not complete (it didn't eliminate their thoughts, for instance), they were reduced to the most stimulation-free environment possible. The brain had very little sensory input with which to adapt or adjust. In effect, it was a stress-free environment.

How does the brain react in such an environment? The answer is, not well at all. It goes crazy!

In this simulated stress-free environment, the functioning of the brain begins to deteriorate rapidly. Many of the research subjects found themselves unable to think logically. Their memories became disorganized. They experienced volatile mood swings, such as sometimes feeling strangely happy and, at other times, feeling anxious or even panicky.

Some of them even developed vivid visual and auditory hallucinations, such as seeing and hearing imaginary things. If they had been diagnosed at that time, they would have been diagnosed as psychotic—"crazy."

While it is apparent that levels of stress amounting to sensory overload lead to "distress," it is accurate to say that sensory deprivation (no stress) is also distressful. In colloquial terms, it is called "boredom."

Finding Your "PEP" Zone What then is the answer? If too much stress is bad and too little stress is bad, there must be something in the middle that is good. There is, and I call it your "PEP" zone. Your Peak Efficiency Performance zone. It is the level of stress under which you function most perfectly; your optimal lifestyle.

However, no behavioral scientist is going to discover this magical zone and prescribe it for everyone. Unfortunately, finding it is not as simple as that. It's not that simple because it is different for everyone. The "PEP" zone is not a specific level of stress. It is a "zone," a range existing between the two extremes of stressfulness. It is defined by the scope and effectiveness of your coping skills and your tolerance for multiple stimulation.

At the upper end of the zone are people I like to characterize as "Indy Racers." These are individuals who thrive on a level of activity and stimulation that would kill someone else. They aren't "hyper" people. "Hyper" individuals may always be active, but they are not productive. "Racers" are people who actually function better when they are operating under multiple demands and rapid change. Their efficiency suffers in a steady, routine, predictable environment.

Then, there are the people I think of as "Family Sedans." "Sedans" are people who would go crazy with the lifestyle the "Racer" loves. Instead, they require the steady, routine, predictable environment the "Racer" hates. When life is moving along in an organized, calculated fashion, "Sedans" are at their best.

If you have an "Indy Racer," you will ruin the engine driving it like a "Family Sedan." And if you have a "Family Sedan," you will reduce it to scrap metal by driving it like an "Indy Racer."

There are advantages and disadvantages to both. "Racers" don't accommodate well to routine, domestic trips, while "Sedans" aren't adapted to high speeds on a fast track. Some people are built for comfort, and others for speed. Find out which model you are and drive accordingly. Neither one is better than the other; they are just different. (Unfortunately, they always seem to marry each other.)

While one of these extremes may characterize you, most people are somewhere in the middle of these polarities. When you find the unique combination of "Racer" and "Sedan" best describing you, you will have found your "PEP" zone.

I don't know what your "PEP" zone is, but chances are you do. Think back. At what point in your life did you feel that you were functioning at, or near, your optimal level? Were things calm and stable around you as you worked in a steady, methodical way? Or, was the joint jumpin' with energy, activity, and constant variation as you juggled your challenging schedule?

Your "PEP" zone will be the combination of variation and stability at which you are most productive. When you find your "PEP" zone, you will discover that increasing or decreasing your activity level by very much will decrease your efficiency.

Finding a level of activity that you enjoy is not necessarily the same as finding your "PEP" zone. Some people seem to enjoy high levels of activity, but they are not productive. They use activity as a form of denial by which they avoid conscious and unconscious anxieties. While you will probably enjoy the level of activity found in your "PEP" zone, that is not enough. It must also be the zone of maximum productivity for you.

Can Your "PEP" Zone Change? I am frequently asked: "Can a 'Racer' become a 'Sedan,' or vice versa?" Usually it is asked by a spouse who wants their mate to learn to either slow down or speed up.

There is evidence that while it is possible for "Sedans" to change and be more like "Racers," it is improbable that "Racers" will ever learn to become "Sedans." The research suggests you may learn to increase your tolerance and liking for higher levels of activity and stimulation, but you will probably never become accustomed to lower levels. Don't ever put a "Racer" in a job requiring a "Sedan;" and don't ever marry a "Racer" unless you are prepared to modify your engine.

"Racers" just don't do well in a slow-paced environment. They may put on their brakes and slow down a little for temporary situations, but they can't do it permanently. This could be a partial explanation for why some retired people decompensate so rapidly after retirement. They are "Racers" who must be on the track and cannot tolerate the "pits."

For the "Sedan" then, changing your "PEP" zone is possible. It requires a slow, progressive adaptation to incremental changes in intensity levels, moving in the desired direction. The degree of change possible varies so much from person to person, it becomes a matter of trial and error to discover your limits.

The "PEP" Zone for Everyone I said I don't know what your "PEP" zone is. It's true, I don't, and yet in one sense I believe I do. I strongly believe that your "PEP" zone, your optimal level of functioning, is when you are loving.

Whatever level of activity you work best at, it is enhanced when you are loving. When you are feeling love, don't things seem to run more smoothly? Little problems stay little, and you find it easier to keep a healthy perspective. Love increases tolerance levels and facilitates the process of adaptation.

As you have learned, feelings of isolation and impotence are two of the major causes of vulnerability to stress. When you love yourself as well as others, it is almost impossible to feel isolated and impotent. A loving attitude makes you more acceptable and more accepting.

Love is the tonic that prevents stress from becoming "distress." It causes the body's biochemistry to be sound and promotes a vigorous and wholesome mental attitude. An attitude of love is the lubrication for your engine that keeps it running in the "PEP" zone.

Stress Strategy #12

Determine what your "PEP" zone is and keep your activity level within it.

Love Conquers "Distress"   A few years ago, I was attracted to an article that was carried by the national wire services. The headline read, "Good Samaritan Not Expected To Live."

The story told about a young fellow in New York who went to a party where he met another young man who was down on his luck. He had lost his job, had no money, and nowhere to stay. Our "good samaritan" offered to let him sleep on the couch in his small apartment until he was back on his feet. The needy young man accepted gratefully and went home with him that night.

181

Unknown to the "good samaritan," his new roommate was a paranoid schizophrenic. (This very serious mental illness is characterized by periods of seeming lucidity, but may be punctuated with unpredictable episodes of violence.)

That first night, his new roommate had a psychotic episode. He went to the kitchen, got a butcher knife, went into the "good samaritan's" bedroom and began to methodically stab his sleeping body. By the time neighbors responded to the screams for help, the young man had been stabbed over forty times.

Rushed to the hospital emergency room, he was quickly treated, but was given no chance to live. No single wound was fatal, but his body had been severely stressed by the trauma of multiple stab wounds. The papers heard of the story, and it resulted in the headline that had captured my attention.

The next morning, surprisingly, he was still alive. The papers continued their coverage with the headline, "Good Samaritan Lingers Near Death's Door."

Another day passed, and still he lay at the brink of death, holding on to life by the merest thread. Now the national news services picked up the story, and newspapers carried it all across the country. Every morning, thousands of Americans, like me, would grab their paper to see if the "good samaritan" was still alive. He had been adopted by the nation, and people everywhere were hoping and praying for his survival.

Several days passed before he finally began to show signs of recovery. A few more days went by and it was announced that he was expected to live. The hospital staff—the doctors and nurses who had treated him—all gathered happily at his room as his physician went in to tell him he would live.

The doctor went to his bedside and said, "Son, I have some good news for you. We didn't think you were going to make it for a while, but you're going to be all right. You're going to live." The young man, beaming a smile of gratitude, declared, "Doc, I just can't tell you how grateful I am. I'll never be able to thank you and the others enough for saving my life."

Discomfited, the doctor disclaimed, "I appreciate your gratitude, but the others and I are not the reason you are alive." The young man stuttered his confusion, "Well then, what, . . . who? . . ."

The doctor explained. "When you arrived at the emergency room, your body had been so badly traumatized by the assault, all I could do was sew up the wounds and put some blood in you. I never really believed you would recover. Your body had just suffered too much injury.

But, in spite of that, you did live. I know why, and I want to tell you. All the days you were lying in a semi-comatose state, the nurses and I could see your lips moving. We were curious to know what you were trying to say, and we bent over to listen."

"I don't remember saying anything," the young man muttered. "I'll tell you what you said," the doctor offered. "You kept repeating, over and over again, 'I forgive you Bill, I forgive you Bill, I forgive you Bill.'"

By now, you have probably guessed that Bill was the name of the psychotic stranger the young man had befriended.

The doctor continued earnestly. "Son, the energy it would have taken you to hate that man, for even a moment, would have taken the last bit of energy that was keeping you alive. No doctor or nurse saved your life. Your love and forgiveness are why you are alive today."

What a lesson! Let's love each other and live forever. That's the best way to go from "Uptight" to "All Right."

A Reminder

Remember, some stress is unavoidable and even necessary. You can manage the excess stress in your life by remembering and applying the strategies listed below:

STRATEGIES FOR STRESS

#1. THE ABILITY TO MAKE AND MAINTAIN LOVING RELATIONSHIPS IS THE SINGLE BEST THING YOU CAN DO TO STRESSPROOF YOUR PERSONALITY.

The ability to give and receive love operates as an immune system which acts as the foundation of any stress-management program.

#2. DON'T RESIST CHANGE BLINDLY. DEVELOP THE FLEXIBILITY TO ADAPT.

Resistance increases the potential of stress to become "distress." The healthiest people tend to be the most flexible people.

#3. LEARN TO RECOGNIZE THE EARLY WARNING SIGNALS OF BURNOUT AND TAKE IMMEDIATE ACTION.

Recognizing that you are on the verge of burnout will permit you to make health-saving changes that will be more difficult if burnout continues.

#4. DEVELOP MORE COPING SKILLS THAN YOU THINK YOU WILL EVER NEED.

Multiple coping skills increase your ability to adjust and reduces resistance.

#5. SAVE YOUR STRESS-COPING ENERGY FOR THINGS THAT REALLY COUNT.

You have a genetically limited amount of stress-coping energy. Don't waste it.

#6. TAKE GOOD CARE OF YOUR BODY AND YOUR HEALTH HABITS SO THAT YOU HAVE A HEAD START AGAINST STRESS.

Increasing your SSQ (Stress Survival Quotient) is the way to make sure you get all the stress-coping energy coming to you.

#7. DEVELOPING POSITIVE SELF-ESTEEM AND HAVING A SENSE OF MEANING AND PURPOSE TO YOUR LIFE WILL INCREASE YOUR RESISTANCE TO STRESS.

Taking good care of your body's health isn't enough. High self-esteem and a sense of meaning and purpose also increase your SSQ.

#8. ONLY ACCEPT RESPONSIBILITY FOR THOSE STRESSORS THAT HAVE TO BE DONE BY YOU, AND THAT ARE IN YOUR COMPARTMENT. THEN DO THEM ONE AT A TIME IN ORDER OF THEIR PRIORITY.

You can't, and shouldn't, eliminate all of the stressors in your life. Therefore, you have to decide which ones have to be dealt with, and how to deal with them.

#9. EXAMINE YOUR ATTITUDES FOR THE PRESENCE OF MENTAL STRESSORS—ATTITUDES THAT MAKE YOU UPTIGHT—AND CHANGE THEM TO MENTAL FLEXORS—ATTITUDES THAT MAKE YOU ALL RIGHT.

A major source of rigidity is the presence of inflexible mental attitudes. Your attitudes should be examined regularly to make sure they permit the flexibility necessary to cope with life's demands.

#10. REDUCE STRESS IN A SITUATION BY INCREASING YOUR RANGE OF COPING ALTERNATIVES TO THAT SITUATION.

Lacking a wide range of coping alternatives also produces rigidity. The development of more and better competencies reduces that rigidity.

#11. DEVELOP A SET OF STRESS-REDUCING TECHNIQUES FOR THOSE TIMES WHEN IT'S TOO LATE TO PREVENT A STRESS REACTION BECAUSE YOU ARE ALREADY EXPERIENCING IT.

Since you can't always avoid "distress," it is wise to have a stable of "distress"-management techniques.

#12. DETERMINE WHAT YOUR "PEP" ZONE IS AND KEEP YOUR ACTIVITY LEVEL WITHIN IT.

Everyone has a unique level of stress at which they function best. Find out if you are an "Indy Racer" or a "Family Sedan" and keep your activities consistent with that range of stimulation.

*　　*　　*

The last thing I would remind you of is a paraphrase of the profound admonition of St. Paul: "Though I take excellent care of my body, and learn every coping skill known to mankind, it profits me nothing if I have not love." The ability to give and receive love is the first place to begin if you want to go "From Uptight To All Right."

GUIDANCE TAPE LIBRARY
PRESENTS
DR. JEROME MURRAY

Enrich your personal development & interpersonal success. Based upon clinical secrets, Dr. Jerome Murray's audio cassette programs target specific roadblocks to self-fulfillment, and provide clear, proven guidelines to get you back in control of your life. Add joy, vibrancy, and meaning to personal relationships; increase your effectiveness and career success. Dr. Jerome Murray's tapes will provide you with the tools to change your world.

Programs Available from the Guidance Tape Library

SELF-MASTERY THROUGH HYPNOSIS $79.95
Learn how to tap unsuspected reserves of energy, willpower and confidence.

THE CARE SEMINAR $89.95
Learn how to enrich your personal relationships.

THE SUCCESS PROGRAM $79.95
Learn how to program yourself for success.

COPING WITH STRESS $49.95
Learn how to add years to your life.

BUILDING SELF-ESTEEM $49.95
The road to a better you.

HOW TO PUT OFF PROCRASTINATION $24.95
Removing barriers to reaching your potential.

LOVE AND LIMITS $24.95
A guide to your child's self-esteem.

HOW TO LIVE WITH A LAWYER $24.95
Spouses learn to understand and live more effectively with the unique personality of a lawyer.

Dr. Murray's latest book

FROM UP TIGHT TO ALL RIGHT $12.95

GUIDANCE TAPE LIBRARY
ORDER FORM
A Classic Collection by Dr. Jerome Murray
615 Coddingtown Center, Suite 187
Santa Rosa, CA 95401   (707) 538-0733

Name _____

Address _____
                          Street

_____
      City   State   Zip

Phone _____
              Home   Work

Ship to (If information differs): Name_____

Address _____
                          Street

_____
      City   State   Zip

☐ Check   ☐ Visa   ☐ Master Card   ☐ AMEX

☐ Account # _____ Exp. Date _____

Signature_____

Tapes	Qty.	Price Each	Total
THE SUCCESS PROGRAM		79.95	
SELF-MASTERY THROUGH HYPNOSIS		79.95	
THE CARE SEMINAR		89.95	
BUILDING SELF-ESTEEM		49.95	
COPING WITH STRESS		49.95	
LOVE AND LIMITS		24.95	
HOW TO PUT OFF PROCRASTINATION		24.95	
HOW TO LIVE WITH A LAWYER		24.95	
Dr. Murray's Latest Book			
FROM UP TIGHT TO ALL RIGHT		12.95	
Sub Total $			
6% Sales Tax (California Res.)			
$3.50 Shipping and Handling			
Total $			

Dr. Jerome Murray received a B.S. in Psychology and an M.A. in Counseling Psychology from Santa Clara University, and a Ph.D. in Clinical Psychology from Heed University.

After many years directing the mental health clinic he founded, Dr. Murray now devotes his time to writing, lecturing, and media appearances. He contributes to USA Today magazine, is a frequent guest on radio and television, and has been quoted in publications as diverse as the New York Daily News and the tabloid Star. This nationally and internationally known lecturer is the only person recognized by the California Supreme Court as an expert in communication. This is his third book on personal development, in addition he has produced a series of cassette albums on self-improvement. He and his wife Sandi live in Santa Rosa, California.